MIX
Papier aus verantwortungsvollen Quellen
Paper from responsible sources
FSC® C105338

Laura Kromminga

Gaps in the Impact Investment Ecosystem

Comparing the markets of Germany and the UK

Anchor Academic
Publishing

Kromminga, Laura: Gaps in the Impact Investment Ecosystem. Comparing the markets of Germany and the UK, Hamburg, Anchor Academic Publishing 2016

Buch-ISBN: 978-3-96067-026-1
PDF-eBook-ISBN: 978-3-96067-526-6
Druck/Herstellung: Anchor Academic Publishing, Hamburg, 2016
Covermotiv: © pixabay.com

Bibliografische Information der Deutschen Nationalbibliothek:
Die Deutsche Nationalbibliothek verzeichnet diese Publikation in der Deutschen Nationalbibliografie; detaillierte bibliografische Daten sind im Internet über http://dnb.d-nb.de abrufbar.

Bibliographical Information of the German National Library:
The German National Library lists this publication in the German National Bibliography. Detailed bibliographic data can be found at: http://dnb.d-nb.de

All rights reserved. This publication may not be reproduced, stored in a retrieval system or transmitted, in any form or by any means, electronic, mechanical, photocopying, recording or otherwise, without the prior permission of the publishers.

Das Werk einschließlich aller seiner Teile ist urheberrechtlich geschützt. Jede Verwertung außerhalb der Grenzen des Urheberrechtsgesetzes ist ohne Zustimmung des Verlages unzulässig und strafbar. Dies gilt insbesondere für Vervielfältigungen, Übersetzungen, Mikroverfilmungen und die Einspeicherung und Bearbeitung in elektronischen Systemen.

Die Wiedergabe von Gebrauchsnamen, Handelsnamen, Warenbezeichnungen usw. in diesem Werk berechtigt auch ohne besondere Kennzeichnung nicht zu der Annahme, dass solche Namen im Sinne der Warenzeichen- und Markenschutz-Gesetzgebung als frei zu betrachten wären und daher von jedermann benutzt werden dürften.

Die Informationen in diesem Werk wurden mit Sorgfalt erarbeitet. Dennoch können Fehler nicht vollständig ausgeschlossen werden und die Diplomica Verlag GmbH, die Autoren oder Übersetzer übernehmen keine juristische Verantwortung oder irgendeine Haftung für evtl. verbliebene fehlerhafte Angaben und deren Folgen.

Alle Rechte vorbehalten

© Anchor Academic Publishing, Imprint der Diplomica Verlag GmbH
Hermannstal 119k, 22119 Hamburg
http://www.diplomica-verlag.de, Hamburg 2016
Printed in Germany

Abstract

This study is a first comparison between the UK and German impact investing markets. It is based on a qualitative research method, namely explorative and semi-structured interviews as well as two focus groups. The status quo of both countries as well as the challenges found in the German market are then used to draw conclusions on how the German market could benefit from the UK's development. Results are clustered around demand, intermediaries and supply as well as national context, regulatory framework, impact and leadership. This study concludes to what extent the UK market can act as a role model and which challenges require a 'German solution' or can be met by adapting actions taken in the UK.

Table of contents

List of tables	V
List of figures	VI
List of abbreviations	VII
Annotation	VIII
Acknowledgement	VIII
1 Introduction	**9**
2 Defining 'Social Enterprise'	**11**
2.1 Existing approaches	11
2.2 Definition used in this study	13
3 Methodology	**14**
3.1 Interviews as a research method	14
3.1.1 Characteristics of interview methods according to Bogner and Helfferich	14
3.1.2 Choosing Interviewees sample	15
3.1.3 Data collection through guideline for interviews	15
3.2 Focus Group as a research method	18
3.2.1 Focus Group method according to Langford and McDonagh	18
3.2.2 Data collection through guideline for focus groups	19
3.3 Adequacy and critics of the research methods	19
4 State of affairs	**21**
4.1 Comparing the impact investing market of the UK and Germany	23
4.1.1 UK and German context, policy framework, impact and leadership	24
4.1.2 Supply, market infrastructure and demand in the UK and Germany	28
4.2 Main differences in the UK and German market	31
5 Constraints in the German market	**33**
5.1 Data collection through focus groups	33
5.1.1 Results from Oxford focus group	33
5.1.2 Results from Berlin focus group	34
5.2 Data collection through interviews	35
5.2.1 Data analysis	35
5.2.2 Results	37
5.3 Overview of resulting key problem areas from both methods	42

6 Lessons learned	**43**
6.1 Ecosystem	44
6.2 Demand	46
6.3 Intermediary	47
6.4 Supply	48
6.5 Need	51
6.6 Danger	51
7 Limitations and further research	**52**
8 Conclusion	**53**
List of sources	**56**
Appendices	**62**
I: Interview Questions (Set 3)	62
II: Oxford Focus Group Results	63
III: Berlin Focus Group Results	69

List of tables

Table 1 - Spectrum of Social Businesses (Kromminga 2015) 11

Table 2 - The five types of investment (Brown & Swersky 2012, p.4) 12

Table 3 - Demand and supply matrix of the impact investing market
(own illustration) 12

Table 4 - Structure of Focus Group Workshops in Oxford and Berlin
(own illustration) 19

Table 5 - EMES, GDP and total average budget for social economy organisations
(Hubrich et al. 2012, p.42) 25

Table 6 - Supply in the German and UK market (own illustration) 29

Table 7 - Market Infrastructures in the German and UK market (own illustration) 30

Table 8 - Demand in the German and UK markets (own illustration) 31

Table 9 - Quantitative overview of expert allocation and topic areas from interviews . 35

Table 10 - Sample organisations 36

Table 11 - Problems and solutions from interviews (own illustration) 41

Table 12 - Problem areas in Germany from both focus groups and interviews
(own illustration) 42

List of figures

Figure 1 - The impact investing market according to OECD (2015, p.40) 13

Figure 2 - The Social Investment Market (Wilson 2014, p.13) 21

Figure 3 - Impact Investing Markets (König 2014, p.3) 22

Figure 4 - Impact Investment Ecosystem (Social Impact Investment Taskforce 2014, p.9) 23

Figure 5 - Financing instruments (Spiess-Knafl 2012, p.93) 23

Figure 6 - Phases of market development (Own illustration adapted from Weber & Scheck 2012) 24

Figure 7 - Key initiatives by area (UK National Advisory Board 2014, p.6) 27

Figure 8 - Differences in market development in UK and Germany (own illustration). 32

Figure 9 - Chain of effects leading to impact investing (own illustration based on interview with In Int 2) 38

Figure 10 - Input versus Impact (Morgan 2014) 39

Figure 11 - Adaptability of UK strategy to German impact investing market (own illustration based on König's framework) 44

List of abbreviations

AG	Aktiengesellschaft (Corporation)
CIC	Community Interest Company
EVPA	European Venture Philanthropy Association
UK	United Kingdom
min.	Minute
SE	Social Entrepreneur
SIB	Social Impact Bond
SIFI	Social Investment Finance Intermediary
SITF	Social Investment Taskforce
SRI	Socially Responsible Investments
SRS	Social Reporting Standard

Annotation

To facilitate reading, only the masculine form is used in this document; all references to the male gender shall be deemed and construed to include the female gender.

Acknowledgement

Thanks to Leon Reiner from the Impact Hub Berlin for giving feedback and a ready ear whenever I needed it. A big thanks to everyone who gave their input and inspiration during brainstorming sessions, specially Rory Earley and Anja König.

I especially want to thank everyone who contributed their time and knowledge through an interview as well as those who attended the focus groups.

Last but not least thanks to Malte Forstat for helping me finalise this study.

1 Introduction

"Social entrepreneurs often struggle with the dilemma of how to raise finance. Should they be a charity, and seek donations? Or a business and look for commercial funding?" Mark Cheng, European Director of Ashoka (Oldenburg et al. 2012)

Impact investing has gained a lot of attention in recent years as a source of funding for social enterprises, businesses aiming to solve a social issue. It can provide a solution to the financial challenges a lot of social enterprises face. In contrast to conventional funding of social organisations through grants and donations, impact investing allows funding of overhead and costs not associated with a specific project. The intention of social investors is to generate both a financial and social return. The investments range from the simple repayment of capital to a market-like financial return. On the other hand the measured social return is intentional and not merely a by-product.

The launch of the UK Social Investment Taskforce in 2000 was the first move of the UK government to examine the impact investing market and its possibilities. Since then the UK has had a series of initiatives through policy makers. It is now one of the largest worldwide. In 2013, under the British presidency, the G8 set up a Social Impact Investment Taskforce to report on "catalysing a global market in Impact Investment" (Social Impact Investment Taskforce 2014, p.2).

In contrast, the German market is still in its infancy, with few investors working in the field. The intermediaries matching demand and supply are few, but their number is growing slowly. They bring social enterprises and investors together and often support social enterprises to reach the state of 'impact readiness'. However, the number of deals and volume of the market is still low compared to the UK.

National contexts highly influence how the impact investment market is shaped and who is driving it. Nevertheless, the German market may be able to learn some lessons from the previous market development in the UK. In order for it to do so, this study is structured around three core questions:

What are the differences between the UK's and Germany's impact investing market? Who and with what measures drives the national impact investing market?

Which challenges does the German market currently face?

Which initiatives taken in the UK may be adaptable in the German market to meet the current challenges? What is necessary for them to be implemented?

The first question is the subject of Chapter 4, which presents the state of affairs of both markets.

The challenges discussed in this study were identified through a qualitative research. A total of 11 semi-structured interviews were conducted in Germany. Three explorative interviews with UK intermediaries and a literature review were used to prepare for these interviews. Two focus group discussions complemented the interview results.

The chapter "Lessons learned" discusses the findings of the research in detail to answer the third question. Here the main findings between the state of affairs and the current challenges are outlined. It presents the possible ways how the UK market could act as a role model to the German market, taking into account the markets' differences described before.

The study concludes by stating which challenges may be addressed by taking the UK as a role model and which challenges will require a 'national solution'.

2 Defining 'Social Enterprise'

William Drayton first used the term 'Social Entrepreneur' in the 1980s, when he founded Ashoka as the world's first support organisation for this type of Entrepreneur. Since then "experts and academics have struggled to define 'social entrepreneurship'" (Oldenburg et al. 2012). Jansen lists a total of 29 definitions from the authors of the book "Sozialunternehmen in Deutschland" alone (2013a, pp.39–49).

2.1 Existing approaches

Achleitner, Pöllath and Stahl (2007) define "a social entrepreneur [as] a person, who primarily wants to solve a social problem, by using a business approach". The seven principles of Muhammad Yunus define a 'Social Business' (Grameen Creative Lab 2009) as a business with the objective to "overcome poverty or one or more problems which threaten people and society; not profit maximisation" and "financial sustainability".

The discussion developed around the terms Social Business, Social Enterprise, Social Entrepreneur, Social Entrepreneurship. The finance of such business is called social impact investing or impact investing for short.

While a concrete definition does not exist and multiple terms are in use, most experts agree that a social enterprise is somewhere on the spectrum between social and financial return.

One spectrum was described by Kromminga (2015), as shown in table 1. Social Enterprise is not listed here, due to the focus on the definition used by Yunus.

Social Return	Focus on					Financial Return
low	Financial Independence[1]					high
Charity	Non-Profit with income	Social Business by Yunus	Social Impact Business	Socially responsible/ minded business	Corporate Social Responsibility	For-Profit Business

Table 1 - Spectrum of Social Businesses (Kromminga 2015)

The G8 Report states that "Any impact-driven organisation can be a recipient of impact investment, provided it can deliver social impact and financial return" (Social Impact Investment Taskforce 2014, p.9).

The Boston Consulting Group distinguished between four types of social finance (2012). Table 2 shows an overview of the five financing categories identified by the BCG.

---

[1] A low financial independence describes the recurring need of grants and donations while a high financial independents results from income through business acitivties

		Organisation type	
		Socially motivated	Commercially motivated
Investment type	Commercially motivated	4	5
	Socially motivated	2	3
	Philanthropy	1	

Table 2 - The five types of investment (Brown & Swersky 2012, p.4)

Taking the above mentioned spectrum approach, a new spectrum, including demand and supply can be drawn up. The following figure thus represents the impact investing market with demand (organisation type) and supply (investor strategy).

		Organisation type				
		Socially motivated	Socially motivated organisation, using managerial tools to earn revenue			Commercially motivated
Organisation classes by Kromminga			I	II	III	IV
Revenue earned through business activity		Non	Below costs	Equal to costs	Small profit	Market-equivalent profit	Market-equivalent profit, not invested into social cause
Schematic view of revenue						
Investor strategy	Primarily commercially motivated				4a[1]	4b	5
	Socially motivated			2		3	
	Philanthropy		1			

Table 3 - Demand and supply matrix of the impact investing market (own illustration)

In 2008, the Rockefeller Foundation first used the term 'Impact Investing' (Coy 2014). According to the GIIN (2014), "impact investments are investments made into companies, organizations, and funds with the intention to generate measurable social and environmental impact alongside a financial return". The GIIN further specifies four key criteria, which are also used by the National Advisory Board Germany (NAB Germany 2014b, p.22):

---

[1] 4a is an investment into a business with small profit by a commercially motivated investor. This is very unlikely due to the low interest rate.

Intentionality, Investment with return expectations, Range of return expectations and asset classes and *Impact Measurement*.

The OECD describes the parts of the impact investing market in the following figure 1.

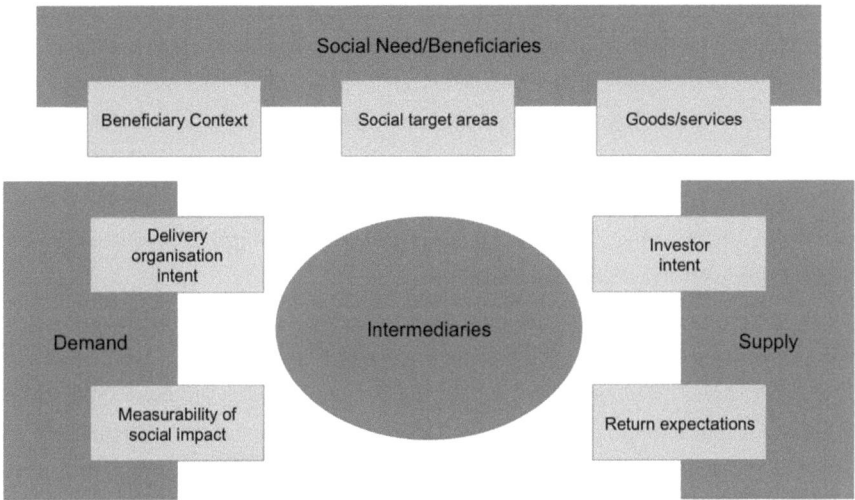

Figure 1 - The impact investing market according to OECD (2015, p.40)

The OECD then used this image to determine, if a business is withIN or OUTside of what defines a social enterprise. For example, a *Investor intent*: An investor which had an incidental social outcome was not considered a impact investor (OECD 2015, pp.52, 54).

2.2 Definition used in this study

The OECD states, which has been proven during the research, that "many players prefer to keep the definitions broad, also as a way to engage more people in the market" (OECD 2015, p.43). The interviewees in this research used a multitude of definitions. Some experts even avoided any kind of definition (In Int 7). The data collected is linked to the interviewees' perspective and required a similarly broad definition.

In order not to confuse the discussion about terminology further, the present study employs the term impact investing and uses the definition of the Social Impact Investing Taskforce as "those that intentionally target specific social objectives along with a financial return and measure the achievement of both" (2014, p.1). The term social enterprise is used instead of social business.

As it is not considered an 'investment into a business', philanthropy is not the focus of this study. Completely beyond the scope of this research is the investment into organisations working in development aid.

3 Methodology

For several reasons there is no quantitative data on the social enterprise sector in Germany. On the one hand the field of impact investing is still young, there is little literature and little academic research has been conducted. On the other hand due to the unclear definition, a clear distinction between other areas of social activity, e.g. the NGO sector, is difficult. Additionally, many stakeholders, e.g. entrepreneurs, are not aware that their business falls under the category of 'social business'. Selecting participants for a quantitative research sample is therefore a challenge.

The barriers to collecting such quantitative data are therefore too high and put the quality of the data in question. The choice of research method therefore reflects the means of data collection that were available to the researcher.

Choosing the appropriate qualitative method is a result of the nature of the research question. Helfferich explains this as: The "choice of method for data collection [...] is guided by the object of research" (Helfferich 2011, p.26). The question explores the possibilities for improvement of the German impact investing market measured against the example of the UK. Both examine a 'why' context and "reconstructs meaning and subjective viewpoints", which qualitative research is appropriate for (Milena et al. 2008; Helfferich 2011, p.21).

Consequently, qualitative research methods not only constitute the single possible way to collect data, but are also appropriate to the research question.

3.1 Interviews as a research method

According to Scheibelhofer, "if one takes a look at textbooks on qualitative methodologies and methods with a special interest in current approaches to qualitative interviewing, one will come up with a long list of varying types of interview" (Scheibelhofer 2008).

3.1.1 Characteristics of interview methods according to Bogner and Helfferich

According to Bogner, explorative interviews are conducted in order to gain access to a certain field of information. The purpose is to obtain an overview and to determine if a person can be considered an expert in the field. For this study, three explorative interviews were conducted with experts in the UK. On the basis of these, an overview of the field and experts for further interviews could be identified and a semi-structured guideline was then based on this data.

To collect further "extensive data upon the expertise of the person" (Bogner et al. 2014, pp.23–25) semi-structured interviews were conducted. They focused on a problem, rather than a specific topic and aimed to reveal hidden meanings (Helfferich 2011, p.45). Two interview types, the 'systemizing interview' according to Bogner and the 'problem-centred interview' according to Helfferich apply to this research.

Bogner and Helfferichs interview types overlap in the majority of their characteristics. These are:

- The interview has a central role in data collection
- Informational, rather than interpreting knowledge of expert; revealing
- Research subject: Problem-oriented understanding of meaning
- Dialog and collective effort of researcher and interviewee
- Active engagement of the interviewer: strong
- Flexible structure, guideline possible
- Include previous knowledge

3.1.2 Choosing Interviewees sample

There is a controversial debate about who should be considered an expert (Bogner et al. 2014, p.9). Being an expert is not a personal attribute or ability, but rather a construct by the researcher with respect to the research field (Bogner et al. 2014, p.11).

Experts were contacted directly as well as through other contacts from their network. The access to experts was facilitated through a cooperation with the Impact Hub Berlin. This co-working space provides a working environment for social entrepreneurs and aims to build a community among them. Through an introduction made by the Impact Hub, many experts could be convinced to take part in an interview. Access barriers resulted from the limited number of organisations working in the German field of impact investing. The personal interview was therefore also conducted via Skype to convince key experts to contribute their expertise.

In total, about twenty interview inquiries were made. Eleven interviews were conducted, which reflects a good response rate. The inquiries were generally met with interest and positive feedback about the importance of such research. As well as the positive response rate, this suggests that there is a general awareness of the topic and its importance to the social enterprise ecosystem as a whole.

3.1.3 Data collection through guideline for interviews

The design of the guideline was based on the data collected during explorative interviews earlier on. This was complemented by a literature review, which added further subject areas.

The creation of the guideline follows two main methodological theories. On the one hand Helfferich mentions that "the need for structure varies according to and within the groups of interviewees" (Helfferich 2011, p.46). On the other hand the guideline continually evolves after each interview, allowing the information to be included. It is a constant development and there "is not a single structure, but rather a identical number of guidelines as there are interviewees" (Bogner et al. 2014, p.30).

The guideline has two functions: to structure the subject areas and to be used in the actual interview situation. In theory the guideline can range from a superficial collection of topics to specific questions. In qualitative research there is no need to ask all interviewees identical questions. In fact the goal is to encourage the interviewee to share their perspective. Bogner recommends adapting the wording according to the situation and the interviewee (Bogner et al. 2014, pp.27–28).

During the interview situation the interviewer opened the floor for the expert to talk about his personal perspective and values. The questions were asked to give direction and prevent deviation as well as to ask about specific topics. Helferrich (2011, pp.68–69) adds that "interviewees do not necessarily experience great openness as a gift but possibly as a burden". Therefore, open questions and closed questions were mixed.

An example for an open questions is:

    How do you see the access to finance for social enterprises?

A closed question might be:

    Is the diversity of investors a hindrance or beneficial to a social enterprise?

The interview did not strictly adhere to the guideline. If, for instance, the expert mentioned an issue relevant to the research topic, the interviewer would deviate from the guideline.

The type of questions in the guideline as well as the ad hoc questions during the interview situation followed Helfferich's overview for problem-centred interviews. They aim to reduce the impact of interviewer bias, since the interview process is influenced by his intuition (Helfferich 2011, p.85). Helfferich includes the following types of questions:

- Stimulus for narration
- Question to remain on topic
- Request for specification
- Introduction of a new topic
- Returning a statement, offering an explanation
- Confronting contradictions
- Guiding questions
- Questions about opinions (with limited validity, are handled differently)

All interviews were anonymised and this factor was clear to the expert before the interview started. This ought to stimulate openness from the expert, because he did not have to fear adverse consequences once his statement was published.

Paraphrasing as well as a low level of intervention into the narration of an expert were used as strategies to keep these two sources of disturbance to a minimum. Paraphrasing can be used to clarify if a context was understood as intended by the expert. On the other hand a little bit of intervention creates trust and opens a narrative space.

The guideline was developed in several steps:

1. Collection of topic areas through explorative interviews and from the literature
2. **Set 1**: Phrasing of open questions according to these topic areas with a connection to the three main research questions:

    Business Ecosystem: What constitutes the social enterprise sectors in Germany and the United Kingdom?

    Financing situation: Which developments concerning the financing of social businesses have occurred in both countries in recent years (since 2000)?

    Adaptability: Taking the underlying differences of the sector into account, what can Germany learn from the successes and failures of the United Kingdom to improve the situation of financing for social enterprises?

3. **Set 2**: Phrasing of sub-questions which can be used to clarify the main questions of Set 1
4. Mixing of all questions from Set 1 and Set 2 and validation by an outside person
5. Elimination of unimportant questions, questions which can be misunderstood and merging of similar questions
6. Ranking the validated questions by importance, again eliminating the most unimportant
7. Rearranging questions into a logical sequence to form the final **Set 3**

This process proved to be effective. In the interview situation, all questions were understood and answered according to their background meaning.

The question "How do you define a social enterprise?" was used as the opening question in every interview. It was necessary to ask this in the beginning to evaluate which part of the spectrum seen in chapter 2 applies to the specific expert.

The constant adaptation of the guideline was done according to the obtained information, and adapted to the level of knowledge and the background of the expert from the demand, supply and intermediary side. After the first interviews, some questions were identified as irrelevant and so eliminated. New questions were added in the process, such as "How many social enterprises looking for a repayable investment are there in Germany?".

The analysis was made using audio recording and by taking into account the source of a statement.

3.2 Focus Group as a research method

The Focus group method was the second quantitative method used during this research. It is a "kind of interview, but instead of being conducted on a one-to-one basis it is a collective interview with a group of people" (Langford & McDonagh 2003, p.3). According to Morgan (1997), a focus group is a "research technique that collects data through group interaction on a topic determined by the researcher". It can be used for different purposes, according to Langford and McDonagh (2003, p.2), e.g. the "gaining of impressions and perceptions of existing services and products" or "stimulating new ideas or concepts" and hence serves the same purpose as the above mentioned method chosen for the one-to-one interviews.

3.2.1 Focus Group method according to Langford and McDonagh

Langford and McDonagh (2003, pp.2–4) Typically, a focus group is facilitated by a moderator and there are between five and twelve participants. The group-based nature of the discussions enables the participants to build on the responses and ideas of others, thus increasing the richness of the information gained. Several characteristics are ascribed to focus groups by Langford and McDonagh:

- Researcher can interact with the participants directly
- Researcher has a considerable amount of flexibility so that questions can be added or modified in 'real time'
- The moderator can adjust to the individual behaviour of participants and encourage the flow of information

An advantage of the focus group is that participants feel secure and speak openly. Also, it is a cost effective and time saving way to gain insights into the views of a relatively large number of people (Langford & McDonagh 2003).

However, the method shares weaknesses with many other qualitative methods. Results may be biased by group dynamics and sample sizes are often too small. Therefore, it may be difficult to generalise the results (Judd et al. 1991). Dominant group members may monopolise the discussion and significantly influence others. Due to the group process, it is impossible to predict the reactions of the group (Langford & McDonagh 2003).

Despite the disadvantages, the focus group method complements one-to-one interviews reasonably well as a way to gain comparable data from both countries.

3.2.2 Data collection through guideline for focus groups

In order to balance out the disadvantages of the focus group method, a set of fixed questions was used and the group was divided into smaller subgroups of four to six people. Due to the limited time frame of the research, only two focus groups were conducted, one per country. Therefore, the data can not reflect the general situation in either country, but it can give a snapshot insight into the national problem areas were perceived by the participants.

Two focus groups with a similar structure were conducted in the UK and Germany to collect country-specific data to compare both countries. Both focus groups were conducted during social entrepreneurship conferences in 2015, in Oxford and Berlin.

The composition of the two groups was different, but in general consisted of representatives from demand, supply and intermediaries in varying proportions. The setting at conferences with a similar target group made sure that participants had previous knowledge about social entrepreneurship, though the degree of expertise varied among the participants.

The first question in Oxford served to align the knowledge of the participants and start discussions. Here participants learned about programmes and organisations they might not have been aware of. The workshop in Berlin had a different time frame and therefore did not include such review. Table 4 shows the questions asked in both focus groups and how the data was collected.

	Oxford		Berlin
1	What has been done to bridge the financing gap (since about 2000)? ➢ Collection on post-its		
2	What suggestions do you have to fill the [financing] gap? ➢ Collection on post-its, one idea per post-it ➢ Splitting into small groups of 4 to 6	1	What issues do you know of concerning Impact Investing in Germany? ➢ Drawing of rough mind-map ➢ Splitting into small groups of 4 to 6
3	Please specify how the idea could become reality ➢ Drawing of detailed mind-map ➢ Group discussion about findings	2	What should happen in this area to improve the overall financing situation? ➢ Drawing of detailed mind-map ➢ Group discussion about findings ➢ Adding of main findings to first mind-map

Table 4 - Structure of Focus Group Workshops in Oxford and Berlin (own illustration)

3.3 Adequacy and critics of the research methods

An objective truth can hardly be the result of a quantitative method as the personal viewpoint of both interviewer and interviewee impact the data. Furthermore, the limited sample size and conducting only one focus group per country is only fit to give an overview as opposed to a full picture of the market.

The cooperation with the Impact Hub Berlin should not be taken as an further source of 'blurring'. It was limited to two points: providing contact to experts in the initial phase and validating the first set of guideline questions. The subjective view of the Impact Hub Berlin thus had no influence on the interviews, they were conducted in a neutral setting and no employee of the Hub was present.

The impact investing market in Germany is still small in number of organisations. In a market study, Impact in Motion names 45 organisations in total (Choi & Mummert 2015). Therefore, a sufficient number of expert has been surveyed to draw conclusions. Nevertheless, the data set is not free of subjectivity.

4 State of affairs

The status of the impact investing market is oriented on the development of a general market theory, looking at supply, demand, intermediaries and the surrounding ecosystem. This ecosystem can for instance be the government by defining legal frameworks, while intermediaries link demand and supply.

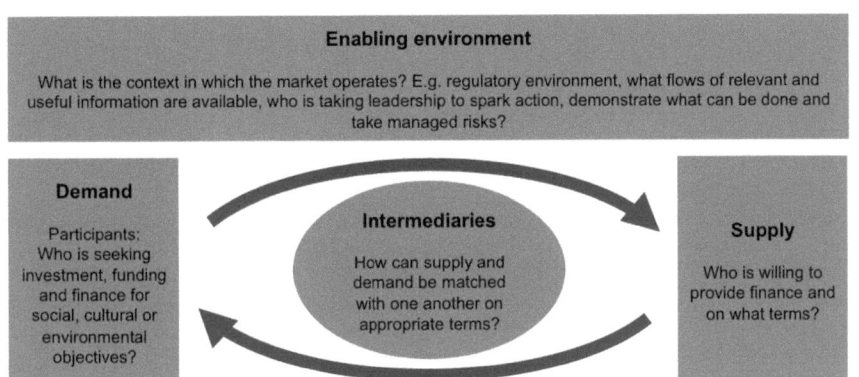

Figure 2 - The Social Investment Market (Wilson 2014, p.13)

This basic model can be adapted in order to suit the impact investing market. König (2014, p.3) has developed such a framework, as seen in Figure 3. König mentions that factors may overlap or might be difficult to frame into one single dimension. The dimensions are explicitly "less clearly defined than shown". Here Impact is reflecting on "how market players plan, invest, manage, measure, and report on impact including the level of standardisation". Leadership is used to describe the "leadership demonstrated by individuals and institutions across the ecosystem as they break new ground, facilitate system change and human inter-actions as well as the level of capacity, collaboration, and trust in a society or in the community of leaders driving this field forward".

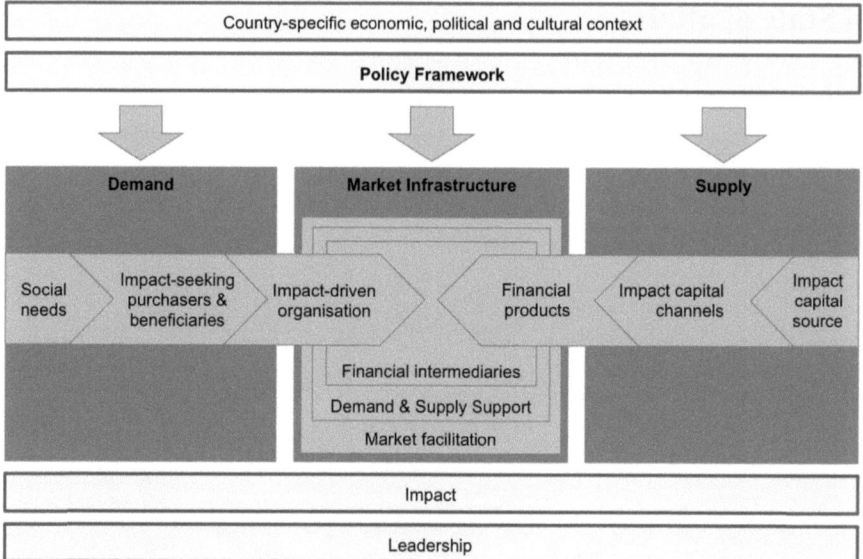

Figure 3 - Impact Investing Markets (König 2014, p.3)

Financial products in this market can be mapped as seen in Figure 4 (Social Impact Investment Taskforce 2014, p.9). Notable here is that the top line is similar to the middle line of König's figure. The column Impact-Driven Organisations represents the spectrum mentioned in the definition above.

The Taskforce includes grant-reliant organisations as well as grants into the ecosystem. The term 'investment' is thus directed toward both the financial as well as the social return an organisation generates. Many authors argue that these two types of return are in a trade-off relationship, where one can only be increased at the cost of the other (Spiess-Knafl 2012, p.38).

Demand			Supply	
Impact-seeking purchasers	**Impact-driven organisations**	**Forms of finance**	**Channels of impact capital**	**Sources of impact capital**
Government procurement of services	Grant-reliant organisations (e.g. charities)	Secured loans	Social banks	Government/ EU investment
Government as commissioners of outcomes	Grant-funded organisations with trading activities	Unsecured loans	Community development finance institutions	Social investment wholesaler
		Charity bonds		Charitable trusts and foundations
Foundations as commissioners of outcomes	Social enterprises/ profit-constrained organisations	Social impact bonds	Impact investment fund managers	Local funds
				Institutional investors & banks
Socially minded consumers of goods and services	Profit with purpose businesses	Quasi equity	Impact investment intermediaries	Corporates
		Equity		High net worth individuals
Socially minded corporate purchasers of goods and services	Businesses setting significant outcomes objectives	Grants	Crowd-funding platforms	Mass retail

Figure 4 - Impact Investment Ecosystem (Social Impact Investment Taskforce 2014, p.9)

Funding can be both categorised as external capital and/or equity (Achleitner et al. 2011). The Taskforce's figure above shows them mixed up in the column "forms of finance". Mezzanine and hybrid capital both combine external and internal finance, while hybrid also includes donations. Donations are often a "payment on behalf of the beneficiary" (Oldenburg et al. 2012). Figure 5 puts all four forms into relation.

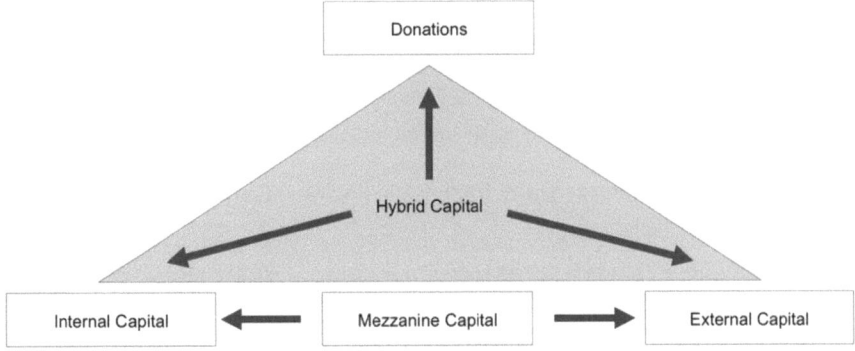

Figure 5 - Financing instruments (Spiess-Knafl 2012, p.93)

4.1 Comparing the impact investing market of the UK and Germany

The UK impact investing market is among the best-developed markets worldwide (Glänzel et al. 2012, p.29). Germany however "is still in the early stage of innovation" for the sector (NAB Germany 2014b). What the UK and Germany have in common is that "the field of social finance is developing fast" (Glänzel et al. 2012, p.7).

Figure 6 - Phases of market development (Own illustration adapted from Weber & Scheck 2012)

Defourny and Nyssens point out that the local context is essential to the distinctive conceptions of social enterprises. They state that analysing the market forces is not enough, but "understanding of social entrepreneurship and social enterprises requires that researchers humbly take into account the local or national specificities that shape these initiatives in various ways." (Defourny & Nyssens 2010, p.19). Observing and analysing the national context of the UK and Germany thus is an important part of this study.

The underlying hypothesis is that Germany can benefit from the UKs development, even though national contexts differ and create a different environment. The following chapter only provides a snapshot and not a full picture due to the limits of this research. It is based on a literature review and quotes from the interviews. (As the interviews did not focus on the current situation, the picture conveyed during the interviews must be considered incomplete.) The chapter follows the model of König, as mentioned above.

4.1.1 UK and German context, policy framework, impact and leadership
Country-specific cultural context

This research cannot provide a full analysis of the cultural context, because of the wide implications this would have.

In the UK, there are more investors than in other countries and greater experimentation with different kinds of instruments (Glänzel et al. 2012, p.29). Research conducted by Robeco suggests that within asset management the impact investing market will become mainstream by 2015 (Glänzel et al. 2012, p.30). This development is impacted by the fact that the UK does not have a similarly far-developed welfare sector as Germany. Social sector organisations in the UK therefore need to provide social services not provided by the government. The public understanding is that social problems need to be tackled through private initiative, not by the government.

In Germany, there is a relatively long tradition of social banking, with the first social bank having been founded in 1923 (Bank für Sozialwirtschaft, providing free social welfare organisations with low-cost credit) and today's most prominent social bank, GLS Bank, established in 1974 (Glänzel et al. 2012). Also, "environmental protection and renewable energy are two investment sectors where there are numerous and quite substantial investment trusts" (Glänzel et al. 2012, p.38). Parallel to that the "Centrum für Soziale Investitionen und Innovationen" of the University of Heidelberg found that social enterprises in Germany exist in a range of ages, reflecting that 'social enterprise' is not a new phenomenon (Spiess-Knafl et al. 2013). In Germany, "a codified welfare system with legally guaranteed funding streams has enabled the growth of a large social sector, which is at the heart of delivering government funded social provision" (Social Impact Investment Taskforce 2014). The general public believes that the government is responsible for social services.

Country-specific economic context

Data relating to expenditure in Germany reveals a large budget, but in relation to the number of organisations, the German budget is lower than in the UK (Hubrich et al. 2012, p.40).

	Germany (in bn Euro)	**UK** (in bn Euro)
GDP[1]	2,480.8	1,801.2
Total income of the social economy[2]	-	46.2
Total expenditure of the social economy[2]	89.17	45.7
Share of expenditure in GDP, inflation-adjusted	3,7%	2,5%

Table 5 - EMES, GDP and total average budget for social economy organisations (Hubrich et al. 2012, p.42)

A 2012 study among European countries, including Germany and UK, revealed that public funding, earned income, as well as grants and donations play by far the most central roles in resourcing social economy organisations (Glänzel et al. 2012). Impact investing still plays a minor role in both countries.

"While social investment is not the bulk of social finance in the UK (in terms of volume), it does play an important role" (Glänzel et al. 2012, p.7). The economic crisis significantly effected social mission organisations in the UK, with public funding for charities being cut by over a third so that charities were fearing they will have to close (Glänzel et al. 2012).

In Germany, "the field consists of a sector of free welfare organisations providing social services with a longstanding tradition of social banking; a field of mature and established

---

[1] 2010 at current prices and current PPPs
[2] based on different points of time after 2000

grant-based organisations; and a nascent field of social enterprise financed through various channels, yet still generally undercapitalised" (Glänzel et al. 2012, p.6).

Country-specific political context

In the 2012 study, in all cases "by far the major player remains the state" in terms of funding (Glänzel et al. 2012).

In the UK the state plays a less important role in financing compared to other countries, like Germany, while there "are a number of social banks and investment funds as well as numerous social investment finance intermediaries (SIFIs)" (Glänzel et al. 2012) Nevertheless, in the UK "public income and self-generated income contribute almost the same share of the budget." (Hubrich et al. 2012, p.62).

In Germany on the contrary much of the "social economy is still financed not through social finance in a narrower sense but through more traditional channels like commercial banks and/or the state" (Glänzel et al. 2012, p.24).

The government is a major force in both countries, though both governments play a different role. While the UK government is driving the development of the Social Enterprise sector to supply social services, the German government is the main source of capital for social sector organisations, but has not intervened in the sector apart from setting up of the National Advisory Board in 2014.

Policy Framework

Since 2001, when the UK government set up the first taskforce, several regulations have been issued to support the development of Social Enterprises. One example is the implementation of the Community Interest Company (CIC) in 2004 (UK National Advisory Board 2014).

In Germany many Social Sector organisations are prohibited by law to accumulate long-term reserves. Capital earnings "must be used in the fiscal year of their generation". This is hindering the development of demand from organisations with a charitable legal structure. On the supply side, legislation does not allow foundations to get involved in risky investments, to ensure capital preservation (Kapitalerhaltungsgrundsatz). Additionally, the 'Zuwendungsrecht' (legislation for funding of free social welfare organisations) allocates public funding to the large welfare organisations. This creates a lack of public funding for new and small organisation and puts them at a disadvantage (Glänzel et al. 2012, pp.11–25). These regulations may influence the revenue generation, which is relatively small among German Social Enterprises, with more than 50% earning less than € 250.000 (Spiess-Knafl et al. 2013).

The UK government introduced two tax reliefs in 2002 (Community Investment Tax Relief) and 2014 (Social Investment Tax Relief), the second extending the existing tax relief on donations to all "qualified social organisations" (UK National Advisory Board 2014). In

Germany, "legally registered charitable organisations are exempted from a number of taxes (corporate taxes, industrial tax and where they undertake economic activities, a proportion of sales tax" (Glänzel et al. 2012, p.39). This only applies to Social Enterprises as long as they use a charitable legal form.

Impact

Social Impact Bonds, which by definition include an impact assessment, remain complex and costly in design and management. Since the launch of the first SIB, 16 new SIBs have been issues. "Outcome metrics and benchmarks can be difficult to define and development costs remain high" (UK National Advisory Board 2014, p.10)

There is only one SIB active in Germany at the moment. The most used tool for reporting on social return is the Social Reporting Standard (SRS). Organisations use it on a voluntary basis as part of their annual statement. According to one expert, the large welfare organisation orientate themselves on the SRS as well (In Int 5).

The overall impact and implication the impact investing market has on either country remains uncertain due to a lack of research and a wide range of differing measurement methods.

Leadership

Successive UK governments have made the development of a social investment market a key third sector policy priority over the last decade. This especially addressed mission-driven organisations, dealing with cash flow difficulties or difficulties in finding investment for growth and development (Glänzel et al. 2012, p.30). The government has played a key role in shaping and growing the social investment market. The government initiatives where included in all three aspects: supply, demand and intermediaries as the following figure 7 shows.

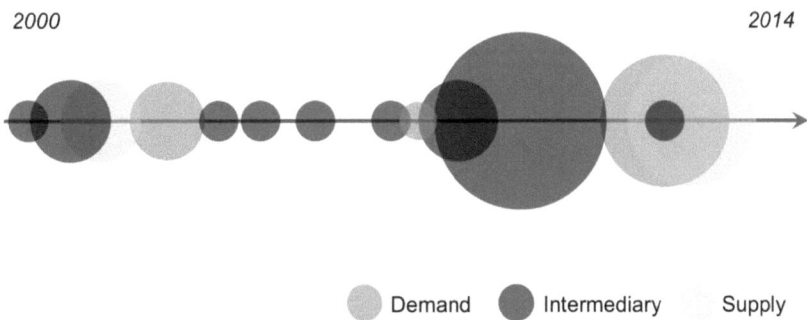

Figure 7 - Key initiatives by area (UK National Advisory Board 2014, p.6)

In Germany the development of the impact investing market does not happen under the leadership of the government, it is rather a civil society movement carried by single individuals and organisations.

Mixed sources of finance

Mixed finance is the norm in the UK as it aims to "fill the gap between traditional grants and mainstream finance" (Glänzel et al. 2012, p.30). In "the last two decades, there has been a significant shift away from grants towards service contracts" by the government (Glänzel et al. 2012, p.30). The growing strain on public sector resources has led to greater pressure on voluntary organisations to become less reliant on a single stream of income (Glänzel et al. 2012, p.31).

In Germany the biggest supplier of capital is the government, which can be explained by Germany being a "corporatist welfare regime [...]." (Hubrich et al. 2012, p.62). The three most important funding sources – the state, earned income and philanthropy – "exist in relatively unrelated parallel worlds with their respective peculiarities and specific funding requirements". And these requirements often exclude one another (Glänzel et al. 2012, p.24; Friemel & Oldenburg 2013). This results in "the combined costs for fundraising and acquiring finance in the social finance sector are far higher than the costs of conventional finance" (Glänzel et al. 2012, p.24). Nevertheless using multiple sources of finance is the norm (Spiess-Knafl et al. 2013). There is no 'common way' of mixing finance, but it depends on the individual social enterprise (In Int 5 and Jansen 2013b, p.88).

4.1.2 Supply, market infrastructure and demand in the UK and Germany

The following tables provide a brief overview of the supply, market infrastructure and demand in the UK and Germany.

Supply		
	Germany	**UK**
Social Banks	3 social banks identified: GLS, Bank für Sozialwirtschaft, Freie Gemeinschaftsbank BCL[1]	4 social banks: Triodos Bank, Charity Bank, Ecology Building Society, Unity Trust Bank[1]
Impact Funds / VPOs	No. of VP funds: 11[1] three Social Venture Capital Fonds are currently active: BonVenture, Tengelmann Social Venture and Ananda (previously Social Venture Fund). They manage about € 40m and offer capital between € 200,000 to 1,5m Until 2013, they made a total of 29 investments.[2] FASE (created by Ashoka Germany) is the only investor in the range of € 150,000 to 450,000 (growth)[4]	No. of VP funds: 40[1] First: Bridges Ventures & Charity Bank in 2002[3] Largest: Big Society Capital in 2012[4] A number of funds: Big Issue Invest, the Social Investment Business; CAF Venturesome; Bridget Ventures, Impact Ventures UK[1] LGT Venture Philanthropy: Resonance which manages 2 social impact funds[1]
Other types of SIFIs	No. of known MFIs: 70[4] Grant Providers: 7[4] Social Loan Providers: 5[4] Crowdfunding: 11[4] Impact Asset Managers: 2[4]	There are currently about 60 active CDFIs operating across the UK - of these 19 are engaged in social investment[1] Business angel co-investment fund for social enterprises[1]
Main Foundations providing funding for SEs	A number of foundations and family offices are engaged in (venture) philanthropy / social investment e.g. Bertelsmann Stiftung[1]	Philanthropy is a key source of finance for the social investment sector[1]
Commercial banks with specific product lines for SEs	Deutsche Bank AG, Credit Suisse, UBS, Lombard Odier[2]	Deutsche Bank Impact Investment Fund[1] The Royal Bank of Scotland[1]
Public-sector investors	KfW Group: DEG, IPEX, KfW Development Bank[2] Federal Ministry for Economic Cooperation and Development (BMZ) Federal Ministry for the Environment, Nature Conservation, Building and Nuclear Safety (BMUB)[2]	-
Estimated Market size*	Estimated size: € 24m market volume as the sum of key SII investors in 2012[5]	Estimated market size: 165m Pound (survey of 78 SIFIs in 2010)[6] More than 80% of government funding received by charities is now in the form of contracts for delivering services rather than grants, reaching over £ 11bn per year in 2011/2012[7]

Table 6 - Supply in the German and UK market (own illustration)

---

[1] (Spiess-Knafl & Jansen 2013)
[2] (NAB Germany 2014a)
[3] (UK National Advisory Board 2014)
[4] (Choi & Mummert 2015)
[5] (Weber & Scheck 2012)
[6] (Brown & Norman 2011)
[7] (Social Impact Investment Taskforce 2014)

Market Infrastructure		
	Germany	UK
Specialised financial instruments	The Benckiser Foundation runs Germany's first Social Impact Bond under the name 'Juvat'[1] Experts mentioned pay-for-success methods, currently implemented or planned.[2]	Social impact bonds[2] First Impact Bond in 2010[3]
Role of Government	As a conservative welfare regime, the state has traditionally played important role in provision and financing of social services[2]	Government (Social Investment Taskforce) in the lead since 2000[3] Government is actively supporting the development of social investment market. It launched the Big Society Capital with capital of £ 600m with which to help build the sector.[2] Introduction of tax incentives for certain types of social investments in 2014[3]
Key trends / recent developments	Forum Nachhaltige Geldanlagen (FNG) estimates market at € 84m, exclusively microfinance investments. Impact in Motion estimates investments by German investors/ intermediaries in German social enterprises to amount to € 24m[2]	Estimated 29 SIFIs (4 social banks + 19 CDFIs + 6 other SIFIs = £ 202m in UK social investment market. Plans to increase participation of institutional investors, particularly pension funds[2]
Networks, platforms, exchanges	A social stock exchange NExt SSE: www.nextsse.com[2] Think tanks: 5[4] Investment advisors: 4[4] Incubators: 7[4] Financial product developers: 3[4] Investor networks: 3[4] Example: Ashoka fellows. In Germany since 2005. Since then 51 fellows[5]	First social enterprise incubator/accelerator (UnLtd): 2001[3] Social stock exchange RBS social enterprise Index (SE100 index)[2] Abundance - crowdfunding platform for Renewable Energy Projects; Ethex investment club, providing online detailed information on equity-focused investments in socially run companies and co-operatives[2] example: Ashoka fellows. In UK since 2006. Currently 32 fellows[6]

Table 7 - Market Infrastructures in the German and UK market (own illustration)

---

[1] (NAB Germany 2014a)
[2] (Spiess-Knafl & Jansen 2013)
[3] (UK National Advisory Board 2014)
[4] (Choi & Mummert 2015)
[5] (Ashoka Germany 2015)
[6] (Ashoka UK 2015)

Demand		
	Germany	UK
Impact-driven organisations	25% of social enterprises are looking for a repayable investment. This part is growing notably[1] Reasons against investments are: wanting to grow organically, mistrusting investors[1]	Very indistinct figures ranging from 5.300 to 70.000[2] depending on the definition
Estimated market size	the non-profit sector has developed from 3.9% of GDP in 1995 to 4.1% in 2012, or DM from 135.4bn (€ ~65bn.) to € 98.17bn[3] Social sector organisations already account for more than 5% of GDP in several countries, including Canada, Germany, the UK and the US. In some countries, they employ more than 10% of the workforce[4]	Estimated market size: £ 750m potential demand (potential, found with mixed approach in 2015)[5] Statutory funding of the voluntary sector has increased from £ 8.4bn in 2000-01 to £ 12bn in 2006-07; £ 4.2bn of the statutory funding in 2006-07 was received as grants, down from £ 4.6bn in 2000-01, whilst contract funding increased over the same period from £ 3.8bn to £ 7.8bn[3]
Market size of social economy (not referring to only the organisations with demand of impact investment)	620,944 (in 2007-2011), data refers to associations, foundations, gGmbH, cooperatives, mutuals[6]	300,000 (in 2009/2010), data based on the civil society concept (some organisations within this concept do not fit our understanding of "mission- driven"); 600,000 informal, unregistered organisations are not included in the data[6]

Table 8 - Demand in the German and UK markets (own illustration)

4.2 Main differences in the UK and German market

This snap-shot of the markets shows differences in the sizes of the markets as well as the national context. The cultural context shows differences in the development of a welfare system. While it is low in the UK, it has a long history in Germany. The government is substantial in the funding of social services in both countries, while impact investing becomes increasingly important in the UK. Legislative regulations have been adapted to fit the Social Enterprise concept in the UK during the past fifteen years. This has not happened in Germany, and is the main hindrance to the access to mixed finance for social sector organisations. The impact of the sector in general remains largely under-researched. The government in the UK and single organisations or individuals in Germany take on a leadership role.

The market sizes are different with the UK market being much larger than Germany's, though from the literature it remains difficult to estimate either countries' exact market sizes.

---

[1] (In Int 5, min. 13:48)
[2] (OECD 2015, p.85)
[3] (Glänzel et al. 2012)
[4] (Social Impact Investment Taskforce 2014)
[5] (Brown & Norman 2011)
[6] (Hubrich et al. 2012, p.41)

The main differences in the markets are summarised in Figure 8. Here the emphasis is placed on how both markets developed. The first arrow shows whether the development resulted from demand or supply into the market. The second arrow points out the national context.

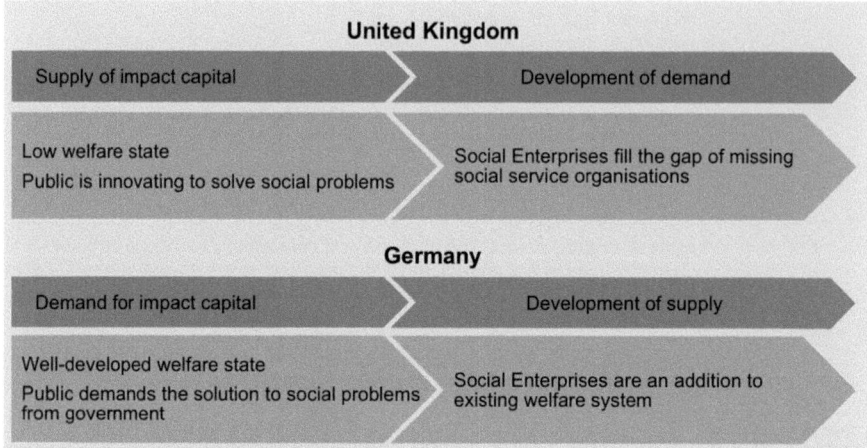

Figure 8 - Differences in market development in UK and Germany (own illustration)

5 Constraints in the German market

The following chapter presents and reflects on the constraints encountered during the focus groups and the interviews.

5.1 Data collection through focus groups

The participants of the focus group discussions were asked to find solutions for the problems mentioned. Therefore, this chapter includes problem areas as well as solutions.

5.1.1 Results from Oxford focus group

During the Focus Group at the Marmalade Conference in Oxford, the participants mentioned six problem areas. Three topics were selected to be discussed further in small groups.

Lacking general understanding of the sector *(infrastructure)*

The group stated that a navigation tool across the sector to scan or assess what is in the market already would be helpful. This navigation tool would act as a new 'trade body' for impact investors. It also serves as a directory to analyse the market (big data) and filter information.

No clear definition of a Social Enterprise/Social Business *(infrastructure/policy framework)*

This group developed a very detailed plan with investors and businesses on opposite sides and the problem of 'terminology' in the middle. When both sides cannot come together because of a different use of terms like 'social business/enterprise', the system cannot work efficiently.

Differences of crowd funding possibilities are not clear *(supply/policy framework)*

This group argued that social crowd funding should come with tax advantages. There should also be a clear and strong assessment mechanism to assess investees (e.g. a scorecard or stakeholder system).

Three areas were not selected to be elaborated on further

- Lack of financing models, including lack of knowledge of investors - *financial products/supply*
- Lack of investment readiness[1] of social entrepreneurs - *demand*
- Lack of networks - *infrastructure*

---

[1] A business is investment ready, when it qualifies for investment, e.g. can provide a business plan or prove of concept

5.1.2 Results from Berlin focus group
During the focus group in Berlin, the following deficiencies were mentioned.

Venture Capitalists *(supply)*

German venture capitalists are less interested in the social enterprise sector. They are more risk-avers, highly value reliability and their general mind-set is not suitable for the sector. They lacked empathy with social entrepreneurs and are "too lazy" (see appendix) to get involved with something unknown to them.

A network between VCs, incubators, start-ups and foundations could be a solution, by

- improving the creation of business models which are viable for investors
- reducing the risk to the investors
- being a way for investors to fill their pipeline of investments
- making it clear to social enterprises which types of funding are available
- lessening the effect of the 'valley of death', i.e. the lack of financing after the seed-stage
- implementing standardised performance indicators.

Social Entrepreneurs *(demand)*

Social entrepreneurs are less business oriented. They often do not act according to a business-first mind-set. German social entrepreneurs believe that "capitalism is evil" (see appendix).

Solutions mentioned by the group were:

- Social entrepreneurs need to improve their business acumen.
- On the other hand the lack of clear terminology is keeping them from effectively communicating with VCs.
- The group said that the social entrepreneur should provide proof that their business model is sustainable and creates social impact.
- The assessment of impact can raise awareness and create a lobby for social entrepreneurs.

History *(national context)*

Germany has a strong history of family-run businesses and a culture of SMEs. These businesses already are social enterprises in many ways, depending on the definition of a social enterprise.

The group found the following solutions:

- New approaches, e.g. collaborative models, are required.
- This should improve the tolerance to failure.
- Change the system into one that is less conservative and risk-avers.
- A lot of bureaucracy and state control makes innovation unlikely. The church, as the second big player in the social sector, strongly influences society.

Legal Structures *(policy framework)*

Lastly, the group mentioned that the legal structures that social enterprises in Germany are predominantly based on, are a hindrance. They were developed out of existing commercial forms and do not work for this concept.

The group could not solve the question whether one of these legal forms should be modified to include the social enterprise concept, or if an entirely new form of entity is necessary, but mentioned that many other counties created such new legal forms, e.g. the CIC (Community Interest Company) in the UK.

5.2 Data collection through interviews

5.2.1 Data analysis

During the course of the research, a total of sixteen interviews were conducted in the UK and Germany. Three interviews, all with experts from the UK, were explorative in character. They are not included in the following analysis.

The following Table 9 shows a quantitative overview of the interviews. The bottom row shows the times experts made reference to a specific subject area. This is only an approximation which was used during the analysis to cluster quotes and analyse if expert directly supported or contradicted each other. Most quotes fall into more than one category.

		Social Enterprise	Investment intermediary
Expert allocation	Number of experts	3	8
	Quote average (median)	23	30,5
	Total number of references	69	221
	Number of references in German	69	152
	Number of references in English	0	69
Topic Area	Danger	0	5
	Definition	0	8
	Need	0	22
	Solution	1	53
	Problem	10	78
	Status quo	58	55

Table 9 - Quantitative overview of expert allocation and topic areas from interviews

The uneven distribution of references among the subject areas results from the way in which interviews were conducted. Interviews with demand were more fact based and oriented on the entrepreneurs experience in securing funding, whereas interviews with investment intermediaries targeted the ecosystem and problem areas.

The debate around social entrepreneurship in Germany has developed into a "core and edge"[1] phenomenon. Ney et al. (2013, p.292) found in a study among 61 interviews that the core consists of organisations and players directly targeting social entrepreneurship (or social business, social innovation etc.) as such. These are, for example, Ashoka, Grameen Creative Labs or Phineo. The other side of the core players are social entrepreneurs and socially motivated businessmen, such as Heinicke of Dialog im Dunkeln. The edge of the debate is formed by players with an interest in or being confronted by social entrepreneurship, but they do not relate or only seldom interact with players from the core. In this research only players from the core have been included. Ney et al. also mention that the core players are not a heterogeneous group and different opinions and interview outcomes were expected.

Organisation	Field of activity	Legal form	Founded
Social Enterprises			
SE 1	Online donation crowdfunding	gAG[2]	2007
SE 2	Work integration, ecological production	GbR[3]	2011
SE 3	Waste reduction, clean drinking water	GmbH[4]	2012
Investment Intermediaries			
In Int 1	Investment consultancy	Independent	2013
In Int 2	Support for social entrepreneurs	gGmbH	2003
In Int 3	Fund and Non-Financial Support for Social Businesses	GmbH	2011
In Int 4	Investment and Incubation consultancy	GmbH	2015
In Int 5	Investment consultancy	GmbH	2013
In Int 6	Employee at public bank, advisor on SME and public funding	AG[5]	1818
In Int 7	Capacity building in the market, actively pursuing impact investing	Foundation	1970
In Int 8	Primarily researching about market, not actively pursuing impact investing	Foundation	1977

Table 10 - Sample organisations

---

[1] German: Kern und Rand
[2] Charitable Corporation
[3] Private Company
[4] Ltd
[5] Corporation

5.2.2 Results

The following analysis discusses the following questions. The aim is to find out where Germany stands in the debate around impact investing and which key areas are constituting the main deficiencies.

- How large is the demand for repayable investments (impact investing in the narrow sense)?
- Is there a lack of supply or demand for impact investing?
- If there is a lack of supply, where is it exactly?
- Is lack of finance a real issue for social entrepreneurs?
- Are there other areas experts complain about?

Problem areas

The demand for repayable investments has to be seen from two angles. Firstly, how many social enterprises are technically investment ready, i.e. do they qualify for an investment. Secondly, does the social entrepreneur want to take on investment. Only one expert could answer the first of these questions and said that about 25% of German Social Enterprises can take on impact investment (In Int 5, min. 13:48). However, the interviews with the entrepreneurs showed an aversion towards equity, but openness towards loan capital. On the other hand the status quo analysis showed that the number of social enterprises seeking impact investment is rising, although there is no exact data. This leads to the conclusion that there is a demand for impact investment, but how large the market is and what type of investment is wanted remains vague.

Experts mentioned both a lack of supply and a lack of demand for impact investment. The lack of demand is rooted in the lack of investment readiness.

> "I just know that the number of social businesses that are attractive to an investor is still very very low (...). It is so low that the investors complain that they cannot find enough good ones, so that they have more money then they can distribute." (In Int 3, min. 15:58)

The lack of supply was more focussed around the 'valley of death', between € 50,000 and € 500,000 (In Int 4, min. 32:10 and In Int 7, min. 20:10 and In Int 5) and early stage capital (In Int 6, min. 43:10). Experts also mentioned this in the for-profit area of Venture Capital and Business Angels (In Int 3, min. 6:17) as well as in general philanthropy (In Int 4, min. 8:47 and In Int 1, min. 20:06). Germany is not as well-positioned as other countries. This field again is made blurry by the lack of a clear definition. If "there is a lot of money" (In Int 2, min. 22:46) refers to true impact capital or rather social responsible investment[1], remains unclear.

---

[1] Social Responsible investment involves market-like financial return and no increased risk.

The lack of supply is also explained by the costs of due diligence for small-scale investments (In Int 6, min. 43:20 and In Int 2, min. 36:30).

The social entrepreneurs report that finance is an issue, but one mentions that building up a team was a bigger issue (Social Enterprise 3, min. 8:55). The other two entrepreneurs did not report about financing being an issue, more so as funding was one out of many concerns. Both the younger business as well as the older business showed great aversion to an outside investor who might limit their freedom or put the social mission at stake. However, the sample size among social entrepreneurs was too small to generalise the result. One of the intermediaries mentioned that "the ones who are really serious do not have any problems with money or talents" (In Int 2, min. 50:50).

Experts were mainly complaining about four topics: a danger of a *hype around impact investing*, a *lack of impact assessment* in Germany in general, *hindering legal structures* and *issues* on the *demand* as well as the *supply* side. Mixed finance, as the norm of financing, as well as the hybrid character of most social enterprises was the root of many issues reported.

The hype around the sector is fuelled by a lack of clear definition and an increased blurring between impact investing and socially responsible investment (which is considered impact investment in the US). This development is made worse by professionals, e.g. the banking sector, entering impact investment and applying their previous methods and reports, e.g. by JP Morgan about how impact investing is a new field where it is possible to generate great financial returns. While the entire portfolio of an impact investor can generate around only 3% to 5% in financial return, one expert states that a single deal needs to involve much higher returns to cover the losses. He suggests that return expectations of a social enterprise should instead range between 30% and 50% (In Int 3, min. 38:38). One expert emphasises that social enterprise is only one way to solve a social problem and it should not be hyped as the universal solution.

Figure 9 - Chain of effects leading to impact investing (own illustration based on interview with In Int 2)

The lack of impact measurement in the social sector is seen as a great problem, also because the state as the largest buyer of social services pays the major welfare organisations by input rather than by outcome (In Int 3, min. 14:28, In Int 8, min. 36:41, In Int 2, min. 42:00). One investor criticises that impact assessment is not demanded by the investors (In Int 4, min. 16:37) and says he would completely exclude such investors from qualifying as 'impact investors' because they show no intention of knowing if they are successful in creating social impact (min. 25:23). Other experts say that social entrepreneurs do not measure their impact at all (In Int 2, min. 51:31, In Int 6, min. 9:29). They disagree on the fact of social entrepreneurship driving the debate about impact measurement forward (In Int 7, min. 29:01 and In Int 8, min. 35:12). Impact assessment is, especially in Germany, connected to the existing social sector organisations. Here two experts say that large welfare organisations are against impact measurement because it puts their public funding income at risk (In Int 4, min. 49:51 and In Int 6, min. 25:20). Nevertheless, two experts see this slowly changing towards more impact assessment, driven by demand from the investors (In Int 2, min. 42:00 and In Int 7, 29:01). The following figure shows the different stages from input towards impact.

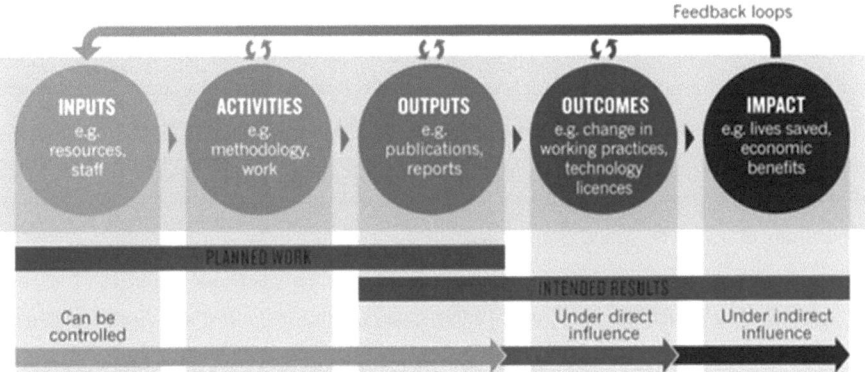

Figure 10 - Input versus Impact (Morgan 2014)

Legal structures are seen as an immense problem by the investors. Most social enterprises have hybrid legal structures, consisting of for-profit and non-profit parts. These parts have different funding possibilities, but especially hybrid funding (mix of donations/grants, equity and loan capital) is difficult to set up (In Int 2, min. 17:04). A lack of knowledge on the supply side is making this situation worse, with investors not understanding the specifics of a gGmbH (similar to a charitable Ltd) or a hybrid (In Int 1, min. 39:52 and In Int 6, min. 16:00). A major problem seen by the experts are also the strict legal regulations for foundations.

> The biggest issue are the regulations. You are practically with one foot in prison when you experiment with the endowment as the manager of a foundation (In Int 4, 43:18).

The legal structures are therefore a hindrance in three ways: They allocate funding towards organisations that do not measure their impact in a transparent way; they restrict social entrepreneurs on how to set up the legal structures of their business, which requires a lot of inside knowledge and they especially restrict foundations when it comes to investing their endowment (In Int 5, min. 25:29 and In Int 4, min. 43:31) and experimenting with it to find out what works in Germany, and what does not.

The shortcomings on the demand side are mainly a lack of managerial skills and especially finance acumen (In Int 1, min. 40:12 and In Int 2, min. 21:19). Also, social entrepreneurs are often not motivated to find the best solution, and therefore they are not working together in order to improve their business or are not prepared to scale (In Int 2, min. 59:08 and In Int 7, min. 17:10). The problems on the supply side are also a lack of knowledge about social entrepreneurship as a concept. In Int 6 (min. 39:08) states that in only three cities in Germany (Hamburg, Munich and Berlin) is this less of an issue. The motivation of investors is not to create the greatest impact, but to "do something fun" (In Int 3, min. 20:03) and is therefore disconnected from the demand.

EU funding as well as donations are seen as problems, because one requires a great deal of administration and the other is disconnected from the real needs of the beneficiaries. Mixed funding is a problem due to a lack of knowledge of the investors on how to proceed with co-investment (In Int 6, min. 49:21) or a lack of understanding for other investors. The expert states that most investors in Germany live on their own planet with specific characteristics, while there is little to no connection between these "planets" (In Int 2, min. 16:32).

Three experts see it as a problem that investors in Germany are risk-avers (In Int 4, min. 10:08, In Int 3, min. 5:57, In Int 1, min. 19:06). One puts this in context with Germans in general being sceptical whether private investors "should play a role" (In Int 8, min. 28:38).

Protecting the social mission was both important to the social entrepreneurs and the intermediaries. Especially social investors, such as foundations, need the assurance that their investment will stay on mission (In Int 7, min. 4:39 and In Int 8, min. 55:53). The entrepreneurs were suspicious that they would loose their freedom to decide against financial return and in favour of the social mission (SE 3, min. 5:40 and SE 1, min. 5:47). They sought funding from their network to secure funding from "someone or an institution that is somehow connected to us" (SE 1, min. 31:00).

Solutions to problem areas provided by interviewees

The interviews resulted in a list of solutions, offered from the experts for the problem areas mentioned above. Most experts had an answer on how to solve some of these problems.

	Problem	Solution
Demand	Lack of managerial knowledge	Open existing support programmes for for-profit start-ups
	Lack of investment readiness	More intermediaries like FASE
	Missing motivation	-
	Other issues apart from finance	-
	Protection of the social mission	-
Infrastructure	Lack of data about demand	-
	Hype around impact investing	Clear definition Defining through 'features' (like OECD, see above)
	Lack of impact assessment	Soft tools on a voluntary basis, like SRS Implement infrastructure Goal: any organisation can create impact (also for-profit) Government should implement pay-for-impact methods (applicable to all social service organisations)
	Legal structures a particular hindrance for mixed finance	Open legal structures (Bundeswirtschaftsministerium) Municipal level is quite open to change Government should implement accounting of risk, return and impact
	Networks between demand & supply needed	More intermediaries who can 'translate' between their different languages
	Government needs to understand greater impact	Government has done this before with Clean Tech
Supply	Lack of knowledge about SE	More Intermediaries
	Missing motivation	-
	Missing networks between investors	More networks (unspecified) and mixed funding
	Investors in Germany are risk-avers	Be guided by mind-set of UK/US
	Legal structures a hindrance for foundations to invest endowment	Open up regulations so foundations can invest endowment
	Lack of supply	Due diligence costs are too high - cooperate with other investors Open pipeline Incentivise private investors (e.g. through tax incentives) Open up legal structures for foundations to invest endowment
	Protection of the social mission	Certifications like B Corp Golden Share

Table 11 - Problems and solutions from interviews (own illustration)

Due to the limited space, the solutions will not be discussed further here. Most solutions were only mentioned once. However, the implementation of tax incentives was mentioned as a useful tool by multiple experts and one stated "I think we can not yet talk about a tax relief for impact investing. It's simply too early" (In Int 8, min. 44:19). Also, some experts tended to find a clear definition unnecessary, while others saw that governmental regulations can only happen with a clear definition.

Overall the experts saw the need to define what implications social entrepreneurship can have in Germany. Which role social entrepreneurship should play is not clear from this sample.

5.3 Overview of resulting key problem areas from both methods

The following Table 12 shows all constraints found in Germany in the focus groups and interviews. This table shows that even though the research method was different and there was a great deal of difference in knowledge between the participants of the focus groups and the experts, the results are similar.

Many of these constraints are analogous in other European countries and have been collected in the Strasbourg Declaration (The European Commission 2014b), the result of a European conference on the topic of social entrepreneurship. The problems found in Germany are therefore not unique, but exist similarly in other EU countries, including the UK.

Problem area	Detail	Collected from
National context	Strong history of family businesses and culture of SMEs	Focus group
Policy framework	Legal structures are a hindrance (for businesses and investors)	Focus group
	Legal structures are a hindrance to mixed finance	Interviews
	Legal structures are a hindrance to foundations to invest	
Demand	Social entrepreneurs less business-oriented	Focus group
	Social entrepreneurs believe that "business is evil"	
	Lack of managerial knowledge	Interviews
	Lack of investment readiness	
	Missing motivation	
	Other issues apart from finance (finding employees/team)	
	Protection of the social mission	
Market infrastructure	Many businesses are social enterprises unknowingly	Focus group
	Lack of data (especially on demand)	Interviews
	Hype around impact investing	
	Lack of impact assessment	
	Lack of networks between demand & supply	
	Government needs to understand greater impact	
Supply	Venture capitalists are 'too lazy' to get involved with something unknown to them	Focus group
	Venture capitalists' mind-set does not fit the sector	
	Venture capitalists are more risk-avers, highly value reliability, lack empathy with social entrepreneurs	
	Lack of knowledge about SE	Interviews
	Missing motivation	
	Missing networks between investors	
	Investors in Germany are risk-avers	
	Lack of supply	
	Protection of the social mission	

Table 12 - Problem areas in Germany from both focus groups and interviews (own illustration)

6 Lessons learned

The analysis of the status quo showed that the German market greatly differs from the UK market. In the UK, wide-ranging government support, starting with the Social Investment Taskforce in 2000, has resulted in a large number of market players. The UK investment market is currently between the growth and penetration phase, while the German market is just entering the growth phase where leading players start working together to build up the market.

In the UK Social Enterprises provide social services and fill a gap, which existed in the welfare system. The German welfare state on the other hand has a long tradition and legislative regulations structure the market of social service providers. Although this welfare system works to address most social problems, some social problems, such as poverty and class divisions still exist. It therefore seams that the existing welfare system is not fit to address these needs effectively. However, if social entrepreneurship can accomplish this task is not clear.

The development in the UK was largely driven by the encouragement of private investors to enter the market. It can therefore be called a supply-driven market development, which may also be why experts in Oxford mentioned the lack of investment readiness among Social Enterprises. The German development is a civil society movement, with individuals and organisations taking on a leadership role. Supply is thus not as strong as in the UK. Here the development is driven more by demand and the intermediaries rather than by supply alone, while concrete data about the size of the demand market is still missing.

The emphasis in Germany, which is counteracting the hype around the impact investing market, is that impact investing remains just one tool among others to finance social enterprises. Social Enterprises in turn are just one way to solve a social issue. This is especially important in Germany due to the strong welfare state, which is already delivering social services and tackling social issues. The basic principle of social entrepreneurship, solving a social issue by using financially sustainable businesses, can therefore be used both inside and outside of the existing welfare organisations. Impact investing itself may become more important for these established organisations as well as for social enterprise start-ups, but it will remain only one way of funding among multiple others.

Many German experts had solutions for the problems they described. This seems to be typical of the 'innovation' phase that the German market is in. The more developed the market is, the more likely such solutions will be implemented, especially those that involve the cooperation of different investors. Testing and reporting about outcomes will play an important role in convincing others to drive effective solutions forward. Anyhow, a wide range of ideas on how to improve the situation currently exists.

Figure 11 is an adapted version of König's framework for an impact investing market, pointing out the areas in which Germany can especially adapt UK measures. However experts have mentioned that investors should be less risk-avers and government should start taking action to support impact investing. If a mind-set can be adapted from another country remains questionable, especially since finance is also an issue to for-profit start-ups in Germany. Therefore these two areas are not marked dark grey in the figure, as their adaptability would need to be proven through further research. Areas marked in light grey are those which may be adaptable to the German market, though this needs to be determined separately for every measure.

The following sub-chapters further examine these areas.

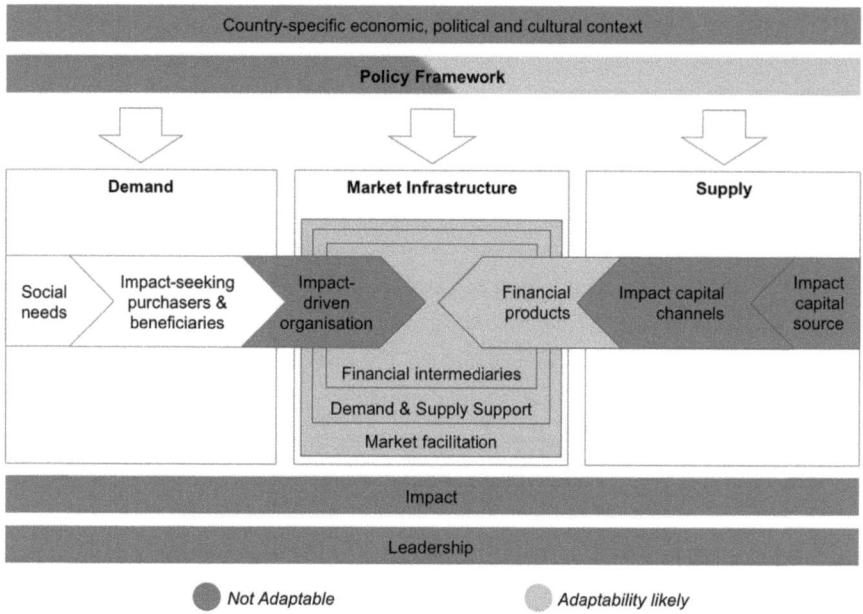

Figure 11 - Adaptability of UK strategy to German impact investing market (own illustration based on König's framework)

6.1 Ecosystem

Since the country-specific context, policy framework, impact and leadership are often intertwined, they are summed up here under the term of ecosystem.

Germany's history shows a long tradition of family businesses and SMEs. Also the principle of 'Ehrbarer Kaufmann' (meaning honourable businessman), a businessman working in a sustainable way and not against society, is deeply rooted in the German work ethic. This shows that social entrepreneurship is nothing new, but has been existing as a principle long before the modern debate about it.

Nevertheless, German investors are more risk-avers. A fact which translates into the for-profit sector in a lack of Business Angels and Venture Capital. In interviews as well as the focus group, experts have repeatedly accused this mind set of investors to be a source for the lack of high-risk capital. Even for for-profit businesses, funding issues are the main reason for exiting the market. This research did not show if there are significant differences between the two types of start-ups.

Compared to the UK, Germany has a strong welfare sector. Existing welfare organisations may influence policy makers through lobbying, though this accusation by experts can not be verified by this research. Still, existing welfare organisations, namely the six large ones, can influence the future development of the social entrepreneurship as well as the impact investing market. They may choose to adapt the principles and implement social intrapreneurship into their own organisation, or they may choose to neglect and therefore dampen the sector's development.

Through commissioning a pay-for-impact model, such as the Social Impact Bond, the government can drive the development from the 'buyer' perspective. It remains to be seen if such models will become the norm in Germany. The UK market, especially from reports of recent developments through the National Advisory Board, can serve as a role model. New financing models, as it happened with the SIB, can be taken from the UK to be tested and implemented in Germany. Support is expected especially from municipal level government structures, as one expert reports. This support depends on a definition, as policymakers need to frame regulations accordingly. The OECD report which clearly defines a scope of impact investing can work as a draft.

Several German ministries are technically in charge of social enterprises: the Federal Ministry of Labour and Social Affairs, the Federal Ministry of Economics and Technology and the Federal Ministry for Families, Senior Citizens, Women and Youths which runs the support programme for 'Sozialunternehmen' (Social Impact gGmbH n.d.). It will be important for the sectors' development if the competence for social entrepreneurship will remain divided or if one ministry will take sole charge of it. The OECD shows that this is not only an issue in Germany, but that most countries divide responsibility for social enterprises depending on the social issue targeted, e.g. education towards the Ministry of Families, Senior Citizens, Women and Youths (OECD 2015, p.74). As they are often innovative and may fall under the authority of multiple ministries, Social Enterprises can only develop effectively if the bureaucratic burden is not unreasonably high. Giving one ministry the lead for social entrepreneurship may therefore consolidate the efforts without questioning the authority of other ministries.

In the present situation, most organisations work as hybrids, with one part being non-profit and another being for-profit. The most common legal form is that of a "gemeinnützige GmbH" (charitable Ltd.). Both ways may be an obstacle when sourcing funding, because they are difficult to understand for commercial investors. Germany is one of the few European countries not to have a legal form for social enterprises (The European Commission 2014a, p.4). The UK is the only European country which adapted a legal form of a company to fit a Social Enterprise. Most other countries have adapted a legal form of a cooperative (The European Commission 2014a, p.4). The CIC limits the dividends paid to investors to a maximum of 35% to ensure that profits are used to grow the company (Drencheva & Stephan 2014, p.6). In Germany the current ruling coalition's agreement states that the government "wants to facilitate entrepreneurial initiatives which result from citizens' engagement. For such initiatives shall be given an own business form as part of the law of cooperatives or law of associations. This shall prevent unreasonable efforts and bureaucracy" (CDU Deutschland et al. 2013, p.78). It remains to be seen how this company form will be defined and if it will facilitate the setting-up and structuring of social enterprises.

There exists little data about the German market. Most data refers to the supply of capital, mostly through impact investors such as BonVenture. To understand the greater ecosystem and the implications of impact between Social Enterprises and other market participants, more research is needed.

The German ecosystem greatly differs from the UK ecosystem. Changes made to develop the UK's market can therefore be divided into ecosystem changes, such as tax laws, and more incremental innovations such as the Social Impact Bond as a new funding tool. Large ecosystem adaptations made in the UK are unlikely to be adaptable to a German context.

6.2 Demand

The research showed that funding is just one difficulty among others. Improving the access to funding is therefore only one aspect with the potential to change the situation for the better. Other aspects should be included into a discussion about how to help social entrepreneurs achieve positive social outcomes.

Further, the research showed a lack of trust of entrepreneurs towards investors. This is normal, as entrepreneurs want to retain their managerial freedom. Therefore there is less demanded for equity than for loan capital, for example. The research also showed a reserved attitude towards banks, as they are less willing to invest in innovative business models. Entrepreneurs tried to secure funding from their network or a type of investor that shared their values. The demand for impact investing therefore depends on the work of intermediaries to connect both sides. They can act as a 'buffer' which can increase the perceived security of entrepreneurs when it comes to their social mission and investors with respect to default probabilities.

The background of social entrepreneurs seams to shift from more socially oriented towards business oriented backgrounds. If so, there will be increased demand for mediators between different types of social entrepreneurs. These can for example be programmes like On Purpose, which encourage the dialog between divers business 'cultures'. Anyhow the data is not sufficient to validate this hypothesis.

A perceived funding gap on the entrepreneur side may be a result of a lack of investment readiness, as entrepreneurs approach investors and get rejected. Both the UK and Germany showed a lack of investment readiness on the demand side. In both markets, intermediaries are working to get social enterprises to the investment-ready stage. These include both educational programmes like On Purpose and organisations like FASE. Increasing this type of intermediary in both markets can further raise the level of professionalism on the demand side for impact investing and soften the effect of a 'perceived funding gap'.

In Germany there are many support structures for for-profit start-ups which are not accessible to social enterprises. Allowing access to these existing structures will enable social entrepreneurs to even out their disadvantaged position in the present market. This touches on support structures at the state as well as the EU level. The current situation puts social enterprises at a disadvantage because they compete with both for-profits and non-profits in terms of funding.

6.3 Intermediary

In the UK there are a larger number of intermediaries than in Germany. This is also because the UK government initiatives on the intermediary side by far outnumber the supply and demand initiatives. FASE, which was founded in 2013 and is the only provider of capital in the growth stage, has gained significant importance in the past two years. The size of intermediaries and what role they play depends on the market stage and national context. The UK intermediaries are therefore not a good role model for the German sector. However, pioneering organisations like FASE gain valuable information that future intermediaries can use to grow.

Protecting their social mission was important to both social investors and social entrepreneurs. Intermediaries can build bridges between demand and supply. They are especially important in the field of impact investing, where intent and mission play a crucial role if an investment agreement is made. Signalling intent and mission depends on the use of language. Understanding the other side's language is therefore important but difficult in a nascent market. Hence especially in Germany, intermediaries need to work as interpreters. Here socially-minded intermediaries with a business attitude can work as a 'buffer' and reassure social entrepreneurs.

Experts in Oxford and Germany wished for a best practice platform. It could present examples of social enterprises and showcase funding options. Funding depends on each business case, and today it can be time-consuming to understand funding models of different social enterprises to compare various options. A platform may work in both markets despite structural and developmental differences. In Germany some organisations like Ashoka present business cases by introducing their fellows online. A common platform for different organisations could decrease informational barriers and could send a signal on the importance of the sector to policy makers, especially in Germany.

Impact measurement is the subject of a long-standing debate both in the UK and in Germany. It serves in two ways, firstly as a form of reporting towards investors, and secondly to prove whether social entrepreneurship delivers the social outcomes intended. There is a multitude of tools to measure impact. In the UK about 68% of social enterprises indicate that they measure their social impact. Though this brings a number of challenges, e.g. in selecting of the appropriate measuring tool, there is evidence that "impact measurement has additional benefits for social ventures: motivating staff and serving beneficiaries better" (SEFORÏS n.d., p.13). Impact measurement can therefore also be used as a management tool, improve employee motivation and act as a steering tool. In Germany the most common method, the SRS, is a voluntary tool to include social outcomes in the annual report. However, impact measurement as a means of justifying social enterprises in the welfare system needs to deliver clearly understandable data on the sector. Social enterprises, especially in Germany, are in competition with large welfare organisations, impact measurement can therefore prove if they are more efficient and cost-effective.

6.4 Supply

The international debate around impact investing is increasingly fraying the definition. Impact investing, which involves the investors' intention to create social impact, is mixed-up with social responsible investing, which is a low-risk investment with market-like financial returns, e.g. green energy in Germany. The new OECD definition helps to clarify the difference between impact investing and social responsible investment. Of what type an investment is depends on the national context, because risk and financial return highly depend on the national market and factors such as substitution by government.

The supply of capital can be divided into 'builders' and 'buyers'. The buyers are organisations which commission the delivery of social services. The biggest buyer of services both in the UK and Germany is the government. Builders invest capital to encourage market development, e.g. investors into intermediary organisations like FASE or Beyond Philanthropy. In contrast to builders, buyers drive the market through their demand. Commissioning large welfare organisations, as happens in Germany, is a way of hindering market growth, as it puts social enterprise start-ups at a disadvantage.

The German market seems to lack unsecured capital at the experimental stage, which is currently covered by donations, grants and equity. As these are a high-risk investment, this stage will likely only develop based on unsecured loans from socially motivated investors.

Investors who require at least a stable portfolio (with around 0% return) are unlikely to enter at this stage, as it puts them at too high a risk. However, social investors who are currently supporting organisations with donations can see this as a 'recycled donation': If the money is lost, it was just a donation, but if it is returned it can be used again.

The 'valley of death', which is covered by venture capital, can also be covered by mixed finance such as hybrid and mezzanine capital. Due to the combination of different capital streams and investors, this requires a strong involvement by intermediaries to bring them together.

The government, as a buyer, can use its purchasing power to favour pay-for-impact financial products. This is the case with Social Impact Bonds. In 2012, the UK government introduced the Social Value Act which "requires public sector agencies, when commissioning a public service, to consider how the service they are procuring could bring added economic, environmental and social benefits" (UK National Advisory Board 2014). In Germany public calls for tenders are generally based on § 97 GWB which specifically states that the "award must be granted to the most economically advantageous tender with due consideration of all circumstances" Section 2, Article 21 EC, paragraph 1 (Federal Ministry of Justice 2009). Here the UK model can show how public funding can shape the market without additional investment.

The UK government acted as a builder, among others by introducing Big Society Capital in April 2012 as a social wholesale investment bank. It was established by the Cabinet Office and launched as an independent organisation. It aims to develop the social investment market in the UK by e.g. "improving links between the social investment and mainstream financial markets". Big Society Capital does not provide grants, but investments, in most cases matched by other social investors. Until 2013, Big Society Capital has made £ 149 million in social investment commitments. The German market is still not developed enough to justify large moves like a social wholesale investment bank. Some may argue that the KfW is like Big Society Capital, but the fact that the KfW lacks the general 'intent' to drive the impact investing market contradicts this. Only one KfW programme is designed for social enterprises, while here the general focus is on supporting municipal as well as social enterprises (KfW n.d.)

Other impact investors can also be classified as builders and buyers. The German market 'core' (check against Ney et al. in chapter 5.2.1) today contains organisations acting as both builders and buyers, e.g. by publishing market research and facilitating the match between demand and supply.

Several constraints keep investors from entering the impact investing market in Germany: risk aversion, high due diligence costs, lack of cooperation between different investors.

Firstly, German investors are said to be more risk-avers. This fact is not covered by the research data, since investors who invest their own capital have not been part of the sample. However, in 2014, the for-profit venture capital market was 0,04% of GDP in the UK and only 0,02% in Germany (EVCA n.d.). This shows a generally smaller market. Financial issues are the main reason for for-profits to exit the market in Germany (Grieß 2015). It remains to be seen if there are substantial differences between for-profit and social enterprise start-ups and how much this correlates to the investors' mind-set and attitude of risk aversion.

Secondly, the costs for due diligence are a hindrance to investments below € 500,000, and mixed funding remains difficult to obtain and retain. An open pipeline and connection between investors may fix this issue. Yet investors "live on their own planets" and an "interconnected financial ecosystem" (Oldenburg et al. 2012) does not exist. The UK market has developed by the implementation of intermediary organisations, which facilitate the collaboration between different investor types and 'speak several languages'. These intermediary organisations, e.g. Futurebuilders, were funded by the UK government. Without the German government's support and will to develop the market, it remains questionable who can and will finance intermediary organisations in Germany.

On the other hand, in Germany foundations hold a large amount of capital in the form of endowments. It could be invested into impact investing, as long as the portfolio is spread among enough investments to reduce risk of loosing the endowment. The current legal regulations are limiting the options foundations have in that respect. Currently a small number of foundations are experimenting with impact investing, but their actions could be encouraged through a reduction of legal constraints.

The UK market developed new financial products such as the Social Impact Bond. Whether financial products are successful in a market depends on many factors and has not been part of this research. However, there is currently one SIB in Germany and the adaptation of more financial products into the German market seems possible from the viewpoint of this research. Such adaptations work at the micro level as they require only incremental changes.

Crowd funding for social enterprises is named as a good funding option by both German and UK social entrepreneurs. How and if the UK will develop further to effectively integrate this tool remains to be seen. It will then become apparent if their model will be adaptable to the German market.

Lastly, complicated legal regulations keep investors from entering the market. They require a profound understanding of the social enterprise concept and sector to determine the risk involved. The German government could reduce regulations, which will also facilitate the flow of funds within a social enterprise comprised of multiple for-profit and non-profit entities. The government could furthermore incentivise impact investment through e.g. tax incentives. Such tax incentives would be analogous to the current tax incentive for charitable donations, but would require a definition and proof of additional value to the German economy. Finally, the government could order investors to not only consider risk and return, but include impact in investment decisions. The German government is showing initiative in reducing legal constraints. If it will consider macro level changes to incentivise investors to enter the market remains to be seen.

6.5 Need

Through the early stage of the impact investing market in Germany the question is repeatedly raised, what role the market can play. Here the discussion splits into two factions: Those that believe that Germany needs social entrepreneurship and those that argue that the welfare sector is already well-equipped to address social problems.

However, in Germany innovation, prevention and scaling are underfinanced (NAB Germany 2014a, p.8). The UK taskforce recommended to "launch a government hub for prevention & innovation" in 2013, which was to address exactly these issues (UK National Advisory Board 2014, p.22). It is not clear if this has been implemented yet.

The above mentioned lack of finance is the only documented area of 'need' which occurred during this research. There may be other areas, such as the general level of poverty, and the higher effectiveness of social enterprises in addressing such issues. But it would require additional research to cover any parallels to these areas.

6.6 Danger

A hype around social entrepreneurship was mentioned by several investment intermediaries during interviews. Both a missing definition and discussion across languages create an environment where it is increasingly difficult to define impact investment. Especially for outsiders, who do not have extensive knowledge of the sector, it is difficult to understand the differences between social responsible investment and impact investment. A 2011 survey among impact investors, commissioned by J.P. Morgan, showed that 75% believe that impact investing is "in its infancy and growing", with another 19% claiming that it is "about to take off" (Saltuk et al. 2011). High growth expectations on the supply side put pressure on the demand, which is driving the market development into the direction of social responsible investment (investment with a market-like financial return expectation). Such reports can confuse outsiders, e.g. policy makers, and put the credibility of the sector at risk.

7 Limitations and further research

The research methods were chosen to give a solid insight into the impact investing market. Nevertheless, this research has limitations. Firstly, with 11 interviews and two focus groups, the sample is rather small. Due to the early stage of the market's development this sample size can give an overview of the market, but it is not possible to generalise the results.

Additional research would be necessary to further examine areas to which this study only provided a brief introduction.

Financial considerations are the number one reason for for-profit start-ups to exit the market (Egeln et al. 2010, p.58). More research could clarify if there is a significant difference in financial considerations between for-profit and social enterprises.

The social enterprise sector still has to find a niche where it can effectively complement the existing German welfare system. It remains to be seen what benefits social enterprises can bring. Currently, different research has been carried out to clarify this question, but it has not yet been conclusively answered.

How many organisations are seeking impact investment is also not clear at the moment. Further research should be carried out with the primary questions: How many organisations are seeking impact investment, are these organisations investment-ready and what type of investment are they seeking (size, conditions, type of investor etc.).

The parallels between the renewable energy sector and social entrepreneurship has been mentioned, but will need further examination. In contrast to the comparative study with the UK, this 'green energy' development in Germany could also be a valuable resource for the social enterprise sector.

8 Conclusion

The research showed profound differences between the German and the UK impact investing market. While the German market is still in its infancy, the UK market has been developing over the past fifteen years, mainly through government support in setting up intermediaries and reducing infrastructure hurdles.

The German market seems to develop by itself; market players have a good understanding of constraints and have started working together to implement solutions, e.g. the recent Impact in Motion report on new financing instruments to bridge funding gaps. However, the German market is held up in its development by national structures. There are major difficulties with legal constraints, - e.g. those which keep foundations out of impact investing - and legal structures of social enterprises that are too complicated for the average commercial investor to understand.

In addition to the UK, the EU also shows interest in the development of social entrepreneurship, while Germany is 'going with the flow'. The national position on what benefits social enterprises can bring to the existing German welfare system is not conclusively assessed. However, there is demand for impact investing in Germany. If barriers are not removed, the market will develop anyway, just at a much slower pace than in other countries such as the UK, where the government has removed barriers and even incentivises investors.

Interventions in the German market could remove barriers, but they will likely differ from those implemented in the UK. Generally speaking there are two kinds of actions: reducing barriers and incentivising growth in the sector. Firstly, with the planned introduction of a new legal form for social enterprises, the German government shows early initiatives to reduce hurdles. Decreasing the legal constraints which are currently limiting the access to mixed funding sources may also have positive effects in the market. Secondly, incentives such as tax benefits for impact investors and the introduction of Big Society Capital, to bring money into the market, only happened twelve and fourteen years after the first Social Investment Taskforce was established in the UK. Germany is still far from adapting such radical measures to incentivise the market. The German national context, especially the position of the existing large welfare organisations, makes it likely that both kinds of actions will be different to the UK.

Apart from 'building' the market, the German government is also involved as the largest 'buyer'. The way that the government commissions social services has been reformed in the UK in 2012 with the Social Value Act. Actions like these could be adapted in Germany with a reform, however the effects are not predictable as part of this study.

Micro-level innovation, such as financial products like the SIB, can be and are implemented in Germany. They are, in contrast to macro-level changes in the ecosystem, easier to test and develop, and the UK can be a good resource concerning such innovations.

In contrast to the UK, social enterprises in Germany are complementary to the existing welfare organisations. It remains to be seen which role they can fill and how this will affect the entire social sector. Existing welfare organisations can play an important role in either driving the social enterprise concept forward or in slowing down its development. They can also adapt social enterprise principles into their own organisations in the form of social intrapreneurship. This research did not cover welfare organisations and therefore further research is needed to assess their position.

The lack of knowledge on funding by the demand side is addressed through education programmes such as On Purpose or accelerator programmes such as those by the Social Impact GmbH. The intermediary structures to develop knowledge seems to be on a good foundation and increasing. However, a greater number of intermediaries, such as Futurebuilders in the UK, could further increase knowledge transfer.

No matter what place social enterprises will take in Germany in the future, impact investing will remain only one option for financing social enterprises. Social enterprises will also only be one way to address a social issue. A hype around the impact investing sector is especially damaging to a market that is in its infancy, as in Germany, because the opinion of a single policy maker, e.g. on the new legal form for social enterprises, can have a great impact. In this context, the media plays a central role in informing the general public and is likely to influence politics. The correctness of media reports, e.g. in clarifying that impact investing is different from social responsible investment[1], is likely to have great influence on the development of the sector in Germany. It will be the task of existing market players to signal that social entrepreneurship aims to do more than simply cut costs, but to increase social outcomes for society. Case studies and impact measurement will have to prove if social entrepreneurship can truly deliver this social impact.

The UK market development is based on a profoundly different social sector. The actions taken include both reduced hurdles to and incentives for market development. The UK government takes a position of leadership, which is greatly different to the current German market, where social entrepreneurship is more like a civil society movement. Nevertheless, the development of the UK market should be watched by German market players. This is especially true for micro-level changes, such as new financial instruments as well as solutions for social impact measurement, as evidence for a positive effect on society.

---

[1] Social Responsible Investment does not involve taking risks in favour of a higher social return

Increased government support, reporting on case studies and spreading usage of impact measurement will be key to proving to policy makers that reducing barriers and maybe even incentivising impact investing can have a positive effect even on the well-established German welfare system. The UK market may be a good example for intermediary structures, such as the SIB, but is unlikely to be seen as a role model for government interventions. For that to happen, social entrepreneurship first has to provide evidence that even in a well-established welfare system, such as Germany's, it can bring benefits.

List of sources

1) Offline sources

Achleitner, A.-K., Pöllath, R. & Stahl, E., 2007. *Finanzierung von Sozialunternehmen*, Stuttgart: Schäffer-Poeschel Verlag.

Achleitner, A.-K., Spiess-Knafl, W. & Volk, S., 2011. Finanzierung von Social Enterprises - Neue Herausforderungen für die Finanzmärkte. In *Hackenberg, H. / Empter, S. (Hrsg.) Social Entrepreneurship - Social Business: Für die Gesellschaft unternehmen*. Wiesbaden: VS Verlag.

Bogner, A., Littig, B. & Menz, W., 2014. *Interview mit Experten* 1st ed., Wiesbaden: Springer Verlag.

Helfferich, C., 2011. *Die Qualität qualitativer Daten* 4th ed., VS Verlag für Sozialwissenschaften.

Jansen, S.A., 2013a. Begriffs- und Konzeptgeschichte von Sozialunternehmen; Differenztheoretische Typologisierungen. In *Sozialunternehmen in Deutschland*. Wiesbaden: Springer VS.

Jansen, S.A., 2013b. Skalierung von sozialer Wirksamkeit; Thesen, Tests und Trends zur Organisation und Innovation von Sozialunternehmen und deren Wirksamkeitsskalierung. In *Sozialunternehmen in Deutschland*. Wiesbaden: Springer VS.

Judd, C.M., Smith, E.R. & Kidder, L.H., 1991. *Research Methods in Social Relations*, New York: Harcourt Brace Jovanovic College Publishers.

Kromminga, L., 2015. *Sozialer Tourismus: Armutsreduktion durch das Social Business Model im Tourismus*, Hamburg: Diplomica Verlag.

Langford, J. & McDonagh, D., 2003. *Focus Groups: Supporting Effective Product Development*, CRC Press.

Morgan, D.L., 1997. *Focus Groups as Qualitative Research* 2nd ed., SAGE Publications.

Ney, S. et al., 2013. Social Entrepreneurship in Deutschland: Debatte, Verständnis und Evolution. In P. D. S. A. Jansen, P. D. M. Beckmann, & P. D. R. G. Heinze, eds. *Sozialunternehmen in Deutschland*. Wiesbaden: Springer VS, pp. 285–311.

Spiess-Knafl, W. et al., 2013. Eine Vermessung der Landschaft deutscher Sozialunternehmen. In *Sozialunternehmen in Deutschland*. Wiesbaden: Springer VS.

2) Online sources

Achleitner, A.-K., Pöllath, R. & Stahl, E., 2007. Finanzierung von Sozialunternehmen, Stuttgart: Schäffer-Poeschel Verlag.

Achleitner, A.-K., Spiess-Knafl, W. & Volk, S., 2011. Finanzierung von Social Enterprises - Neue Herausforderungen für die Finanzmärkte. In Hackenberg, H. / Empter, S. (Hrsg.) Social Entrepreneurship - Social Business: Für die Gesellschaft unternehmen. Wiesbaden: VS Verlag.

Ashoka Germany, 2015. Ashoka Germany Homepage. Available at: http://germany.ashoka.org/ [Accessed September 14, 2015].

Ashoka UK, 2015. Ashoka UK Homepage. Available at: http://uk.ashoka.org/ [Accessed September 14, 2015].

Bogner, A., Littig, B. & Menz, W., 2014. Interview mit Experten 1st ed., Wiesbaden: Springer Verlag.

Brown, A. & Norman, W., 2011. Lighting the touchpaper, Growing the Market for Social Investment in England, Available at: http://youngfoundation.org/wp-content/uploads/2012/10/owing_the_market_for_social_investment_FINAL.pdf.

Brown, A. & Swersky, A., 2012. The First Billion, Available at: https://www.bcg.com/documents/file115598.pdf.

CDU Deutschland, CSU-Landesleitung & SPD, 2013. Deutschlands Zukunft Gestalten, Koalitionsvertrag zwischen CDU, CSU und SPD, Berlin. Available at: https://www.cdu.de/sites/default/files/media/dokumente/koalitionsvertrag.pdf.

Choi, Y. & Mummert, A., 2015. Closing The Gap, Available at: http://impactinmotion.com/wp-content/uploads/2015/03/Closing-the-gap_Final.pdf.

Coy, P., 2014. The Penny-Pinching Woman Who Gives Away the Rockefellers' Fortune. Bloomberg Business. Available at: http://www.bloomberg.com/bw/articles/2014-10-03/rockefeller-foundation-aims-for-impact [Accessed August 31, 2015].

Defourny, J. & Nyssens, M., 2010. Conceptions of Social Enterprise and Social Entrepreneurship in Europe and the United States: Convergences and Divergences. Journal of Social Entrepreneurship, 1(1), pp.32–53. Available at: http://dx.doi.org/10.1080/19420670903442053.

Drencheva, A. & Stephan, U., 2014. The State of Social Entrepreneurship in the UK, SEFORÏS Country Report, Available at: http://www.seforis.eu/upload/reports/Country_Report_UK.pdf.

Egeln, J. et al., 2010. Ursachen für das Scheitern junger Unternehmen in den ersten fünf Jahren ihres Bestehens, Mannheim und Neuss. Available at: http://www.bmwi.de/BMWi/Redaktion/PDF/Publikationen/Studien/ursachen-fuer-das-scheitern-junger-unternehmen,property=pdf,bereich=bmwi,sprache=de,rwb=true.pdf.

EVCA, Anteil der Venture Capital-Investitionen am nationalen BIP ausgewählter europäischer Länder im Jahr 2014. statista. Available at: http://de.statista.com/statistik/daten/studie/167080/umfrage/anteil-der-venture-capital-investitionen-in-europa-am-nationalen-bip/ [Accessed September 21, 2015].

Federal Ministry of Justice, 2009. Notice of Regulations on Contract Awards for Public Supplies and Services - Part A (VOL/A) Version 2009, Germany: Federal Gazette.

Friemel, T. & Oldenburg, F., 2013. Vom Planetensystem zum Ökosystem Finanzierungen für Sozialunternehmer neu denken, Available at: http://germany.ashoka.org/sites/germany.ashoka.org/files/2013-02_Ashoka Thesenpapier-Finanzierungen-neu-denken.pdf.

Glänzel, G., Schmitz, B. & Mildenberger, G., 2012. Social finance investment instruments , markets and cultures in the EU, Available at: http://www.tepsie.eu/images/documents/tepsie.d4.1.4.2socialfinanceinstruments.pdf.

Google, 2015. Google. Available at: www.google.com [Accessed September 18, 2015].

Grameen Creative Lab, 2009. The 7 principles of Social Business. Available at: http://www.grameencreativelab.com/a-concept-to-eradicate-poverty/7-principles.html [Accessed August 31, 2015].

Grieß, A., 2015. Fachkräftemangel verliert für Start-Ups an Bedeutung. statista. Available at: http://de.statista.com/infografik/3764/groesste-sorge-von-start-ups-in-deutschland/ [Accessed September 21, 2015].

Helfferich, C., 2011. Die Qualität qualitativer Daten 4. Auflage., VS Verlag für Sozialwissenschaften.

Hubrich, D.-K. et al., 2012. Comparative Case Study Report on the State of the Social Economy. A deliverable of the project: "The theoretical, empirical and policy foundations for building social innovation in Europe" (TEPSIE), Brussels.

Investing Global Impact Network, 2014. Impact Investing. Available at: http://www.thegiin.org/cgi-bin/iowa/investing/index.html [Accessed August 31, 2015].

Jansen, S.A., 2013a. Begriffs- und Konzeptgeschichte von Sozialunternehmen; Differenztheoretische Typologisierungen. In Sozialunternehmen in Deutschland. Wiesbaden: Springer VS.

Jansen, S.A., 2013b. Skalierung von sozialer Wirksamkeit; Thesen, Tests und Trends zur Organisation und Innovation von Sozialunternehmen und deren Wirksamkeitsskalierung. In Sozialunternehmen in Deutschland. Wiesbaden: Springer VS.

Judd, C.M., Smith, E.R. & Kidder, L.H., 1991. Research Methods in Social Relations, New York: Harcourt Brace Jovanovic College Publishers.

KfW, IKU – Investitionskredit Kommunale und Soziale Unternehmen. Available at: https://www.kfw.de/partner/KfW-Partnerportal/Architekten-Bauingenieure-Energieberater/F%C3%B6rderprodukte/IKU-Investitionskredit-Kommunale-und-Soziale-Unternehmen-(148)/index.jsp [Accessed September 21, 2015].

König, A.-N., 2014. MARKET ANALYSIS AND DESIGN MARKET ANALYSIS IN SOCIAL IMPACT INVESTING : DESIGN CONSIDERATIONS AND INTERNATIONAL, Available at: http://globalpolicy.iipcollaborative.org/wp-content/uploads/sites/5/2014/12/Market-design.pdf.

Kromminga, L., 2015. Sozialer Tourismus: Armutsreduktion durch das Social Business Model im Tourismus, Hamburg: Diplomica Verlag.

Langford, J. & McDonagh, D., 2003. Focus Groups: Supporting Effective Product Development, CRC Press.

Milena, Z.R., Dainora, G. & Alin, S., 2008. Qualitative research methods: A comparison between focus-group and in-depth interview. Annals of Faculty of Economics, 4(1), pp.1279–1284.

Morgan, B., 2014. Research impact: Income for outcome. Nature, 511(7510), pp.S72–S75. Available at: http://dx.doi.org/10.1038/511S72a.

Morgan, D.L., 1997. Focus Groups as Qualitative Research 2nd ed., SAGE Publications.

NAB Germany, 2014a. Social Impact Investing: Financing Social Change, Available at: http://www.socialimpactinvestment.org/reports/150127_NAB_Report.pdf.

NAB Germany, 2014b. Wirkungsorientiertes Investieren, Neue Finanzierungsquellen zur Lösung gesellschaftlicher Herausforderungen, Available at: https://www.bertelsmann-stiftung.de/fileadmin//user_upload/Studie_Wirkungsorientiertes_Investieren.pdf.

Ney, S. et al., 2013. Social Entrepreneurship in Deutschland: Debatte, Verständnis und Evolution. In P. D. S. A. Jansen, P. D. M. Beckmann, & P. D. R. G. Heinze, eds. Sozialunternehmen in Deutschland. Wiesbaden: Springer VS, pp. 285–311.

OECD, 2015. Social Impact Investment, Building The Evidence Base, Available at: http://www.oecd.org/sti/ind/social-impact-investment.pdf.

Oldenburg, F. et al., 2012. Ashoka on Social Finance, Selected Publications 2011&2012, Available at: http://germany.ashoka.org/sites/germany.ashoka.org/files/Ashoka-on-Social-Finance.pdf.

Saltuk, Y., Bouri, A. & Leung, G., 2011. Insight into the Impact Investment Market, an in-depth analysis of investor perspectives and over 2,200 transactions. J. P. Morgan, Social Finance Research, (December). Available at: http://www.thegiin.org/assets/documents/Insight into Impact Investment Market2.pdf.

Scheibelhofer, E., 2008. Combining Narration-Based Interviews with Topical Interviews: Methodological Reflections on Research Practices. International Journal of Social Research Methodology, 11(5), pp.403–416.

SEFORÏS, The State of Social Entrepreneurship - Impact of Social Enterprises, Available at: http://www.seforis.eu/upload/reports/6._Impact_of_Social_Enterprises.pdf.

Social Impact gGmbH, Social Impact gGmbH Homepage. Available at: http://socialimpact.eu/ [Accessed September 18, 2015].

Social Impact Investment Taskforce, 2014. IMPACT INVESTMENT: THE INVISIBLE HEART OF MARKETS, Available at: https://www.bertelsmann-stiftung.de/fileadmin/files/user_upload/Impact_Investment_Report.pdf.

Spiess-Knafl, D.I.W., 2012. Finanzierung von Sozialunternehmen, Eine theoretische und empirische Analyse. Technische Universität München. Available at: http://d-nb.info/102496406X/34.

Spiess-Knafl, D.W. & Jansen, P.D.S.A., 2013. Imperfections in the social investment market and options on how to address them, Available at: http://social-enterprise-finance.eu/sites/default/files/Imperfection_In_The_Social_Investment.pdf.

Spiess-Knafl, W. et al., 2013. Eine Vermessung der Landschaft deutscher Sozialunternehmen. In Sozialunternehmen in Deutschland. Wiesbaden: Springer VS.

The European Commission, 2014a. A map of social enterprises and their eco-systems in Europe, Executive Summary, London. Available at: ec.europa.eu/social/BlobServlet?docId=12988&langId=en.

The European Commission, 2014b. Strasbourg Declaration, Initial Ideas and Suggestions From Stakeholders, Strasbourg. Available at: http://ec.europa.eu/internal_market/conferences/2014/0116-social-entrepreneurs/docs/strasbourg-declaration-annex_en.pdf.

UK National Advisory Board, 2014. Building a social impact investment market, The UK experience, Available at: http://www.socialimpactinvestment.org/reports/UK Advisory Board to the Social Investment Taskforce Report September 2014.pdf.

Weber, M. & Scheck, P.D.B., 2012. Impact Investing in Deutschland, Available at: http://www.impactinmotion.com/wp/wp-content/uploads/2013/05/Impact-Investing-in-Detschland_08052013.pdf.

Wilson, K.E., 2014. New Investment Approaches for Addressing Social and Economic Challenges, Available at: http://dx.doi.org/10.1787/5jz2bz8g00jj-en.

Appendices

I: Interview Questions (Set 3)

	Question for Social Enterprises	
1	How long ago did you have the idea for your company?	
2	When did you start?	
3	How did you finance so far?	
4	In which stage is your business?	
5	What was the most difficult in finding funding?	
6	How do you earn revenue through your business model?	
Order	Question for Investment Intermediaries	Topic
1	Wie definieren Sie ein Social Business?	Concept
2	Wie kritisch sehen Sie, dass das SB Model für Profitmaximierung missbraucht werden könnte, der gute Zweck nur Deckmantel ist?	Concept
3	Sind SB in finaziellen Kriesen resitenter als andere soziale Organisationen?	Concept
4	Welche Strukturen fehlen in Deutschland für das Konzept des SB?	Ecosystem
5	Welche Entwicklungen im SB Sektor sind Ihnen bekannt, seit dem Jahr 2000?	Ecosystem
6	Was sind die Probleme des Sozialen Sektors in Deutschland? Mögliche Antwort: Intransparent, ineffizient, hat Finanzierungsprobleme. Follow up: Sind SB darin besser?	Stakeholder
7	Schiebt die Regierung die Entwicklung von SB nur deshalb voran um auf lange Sicht Geld zu sparen?	Stakeholder
8	Welche Position hat die staatliche Seite bezüglich der Finanzschwierigkeiten des SB Sektors?	Stakeholder
9	Sollte der Staat SB besonders vor Markteinflüssen "schützen", weil sie einen sozialen Auftrag erfüllen?	Stakeholder
10	Wie stehen Ihrer Meinung nach NPO und FP zu SB?	Stakeholder
11	Wie gehen die etablierten Organisationen mit Innovationen um? Sind die Strukturen in Deutschland so fest, dass Innovation überhaupt möglich ist? Was ist nötig damit Innovationen möglich werden?	Stakeholder
12	Wie sehen Sie den Zugang zu Finanzierung für ein SB?	Finance
13	Welche Geldgeber sind Ihnen für SBes bekannt?	Finance
14	Wie groß sind die Anteile von private Investoren, Crowdfunding, Staat und Großinvestoren? Im Unterschied zu FP Businesses, der Anteil von Finanzquellen? Welche Art von Investoren haben besonders Interesse an SB?	Finance
15	Welche Finanzinstrumente kommen besonders in Frage bei der Außenfinanzierung? Hier sind Instrumente, nicht Arten von Investoren gemeint. Welche Rolle spielen Pro-Bono Angebote, Freiwillige Helfer etc.?	Finance
16	Welche Ansprüche an Investoren stellen SBes?	Finance
17	Ist die Vielfalt an Investitionsmöglichkeiten hinderlich oder günstig?	Finance
18	Woher stammt die Auffassung das es eine Finanzierungslücke gibt? Ist dies Ihrer Meinung nach wirklich ein Fehlen von Kapital?	Finance
19	Sind SB tatsächlich risikoreicher als das Investment in ein FP, wie oft behauptet wird?	Finance
20	Mir wird oft berichtet das die Follow-Up Investition schwierig ist, d.h. nach der Idea-Stage. Warum ist das so? Warum gibt es keine Investoren in dieser Phase?	Finance
21	Wurden neue Finanzmodelle oder Instrumente für den SB entwickelt?	Finance
22	Sollte es eine stärke Durchsetzung von SROI geben um mehr Investoren anzulocken?	Finance

II: Oxford Focus Group Results

BIG Venture Challenge — this is also run by others (eg. Clearly So, I think)
Social Seed
Comic Relief — a TECH FOR GOOD
~~Unlimited~~ UNLTD — FAST GROWTH
— TRY IT AND DO IT
Social Incubator Fund
Social Angel Investors → +250k later stage
Crowd funding → Crowd Cube

Support & Money

Big Potential — a grant and advice
NESTA — sometimes invest directly
Venture Philanthropists
— Awesome Foundation
KIC's — european based (eg. Climate KIC) — UCL
Health KIC — Brand
EU Micro-credit scheme

Portugal
wholesale fund — European Union
150 million over six years.

Public Investment Fund
CEI   20 million   all stages
         → Case
Grp. SOS → Solidarity
Comptoir de l'innovation (CDI) → Start-ups
                                → Social entrepreneurs

History Review I

deprived constituencies —

- 3rd Fund: invest in 10% things of social value (renewable energy, NHS)

- 4th Fund: £10m to invest in social enterprises. Reduced to £6m – Fund difficult to find viable enterprises

→ Funding from EU – Structural Funds – available for less developed regions
- Re Microloan Fund – fund into a loan fund (10% default rate)

→ Big Society Capital – can't lose money – very careful about investment

→ In 2000 Phenix Fund { opt out of social enterprise
                       CDFI
  (a one-off)   *
  Support to unbankable organisations

→ Social Investment Fund (run by Co.)

2001
* Bridges Ventures – £10m to invest in deprived 75% communities to start businesses
- Financial success –
  all in cities –
- Retained social impact, not job creation
? Then have fund to

→ Start-up loans – from British Business Bank
  loans up to £12,000

> GUIDANCE ON PREPARATION FOR EACH OPPORTUNITY
> ↳ BOTH INFO & REFERRALS TO OTHERS

> HUMAN ADVISORY SERVICE/NETWORK
>
> ASSOC OF ~~PEOPLE~~ SOCIAL INVESTMENT
>
> TRADE BODY / COMMUNITY OF INTEREST

> - CREATE AND PROMOTE NEW FINANCING MODELS
> - EXPLAINING AND TRANSLATING THE BENEFITS OF SOCIAL INVESTMENT

Not selected first ideas

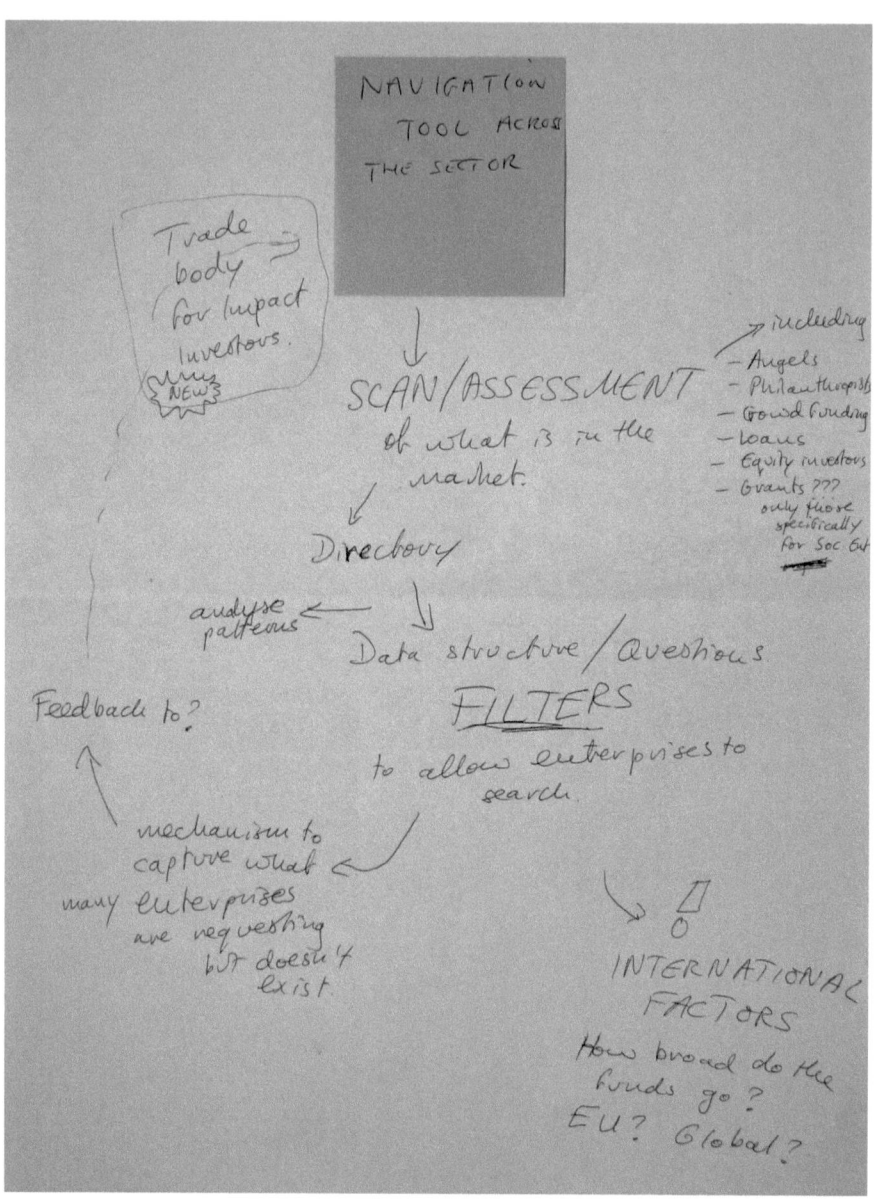

Group 1: Navigation Tool

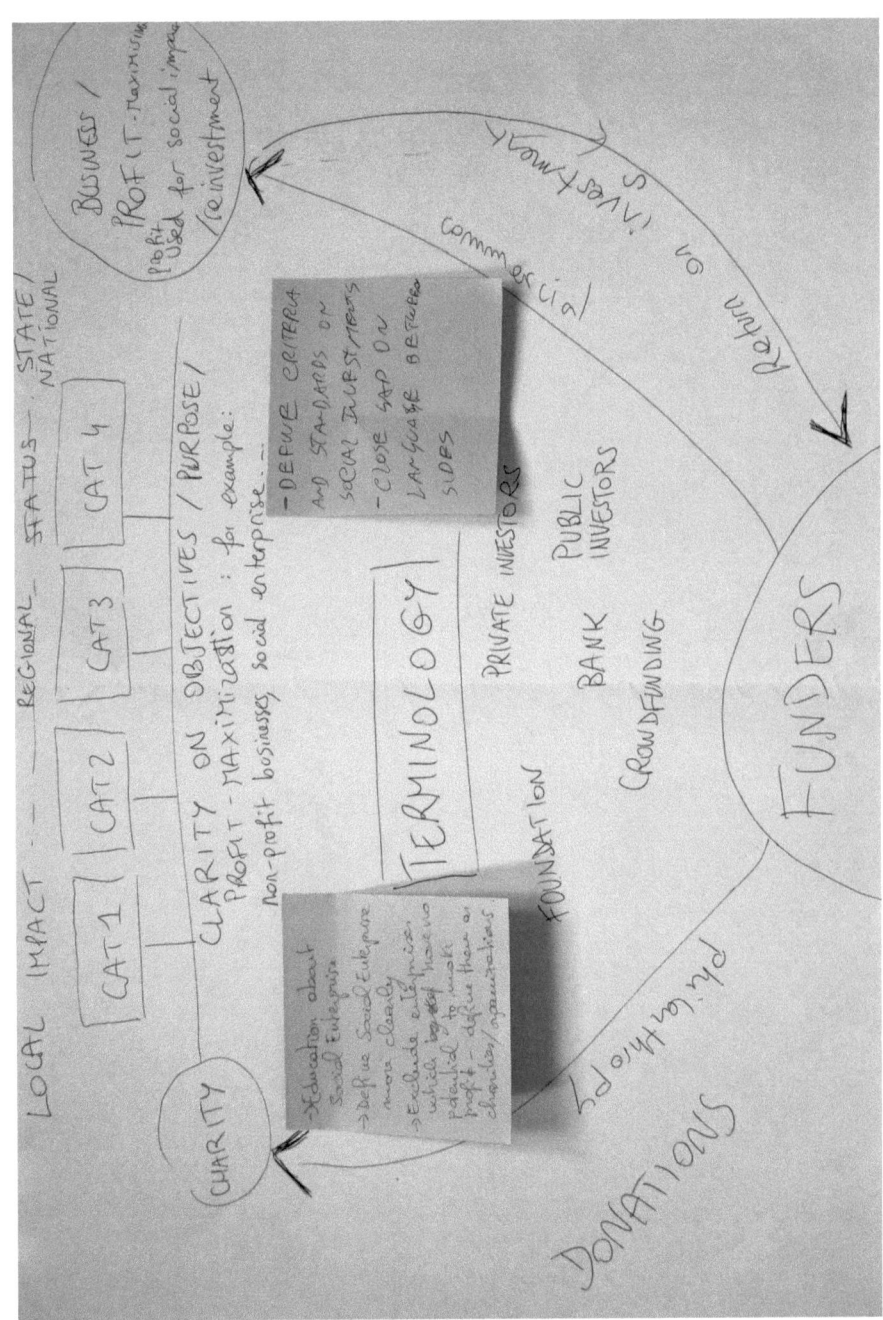

Group 2: Terminology

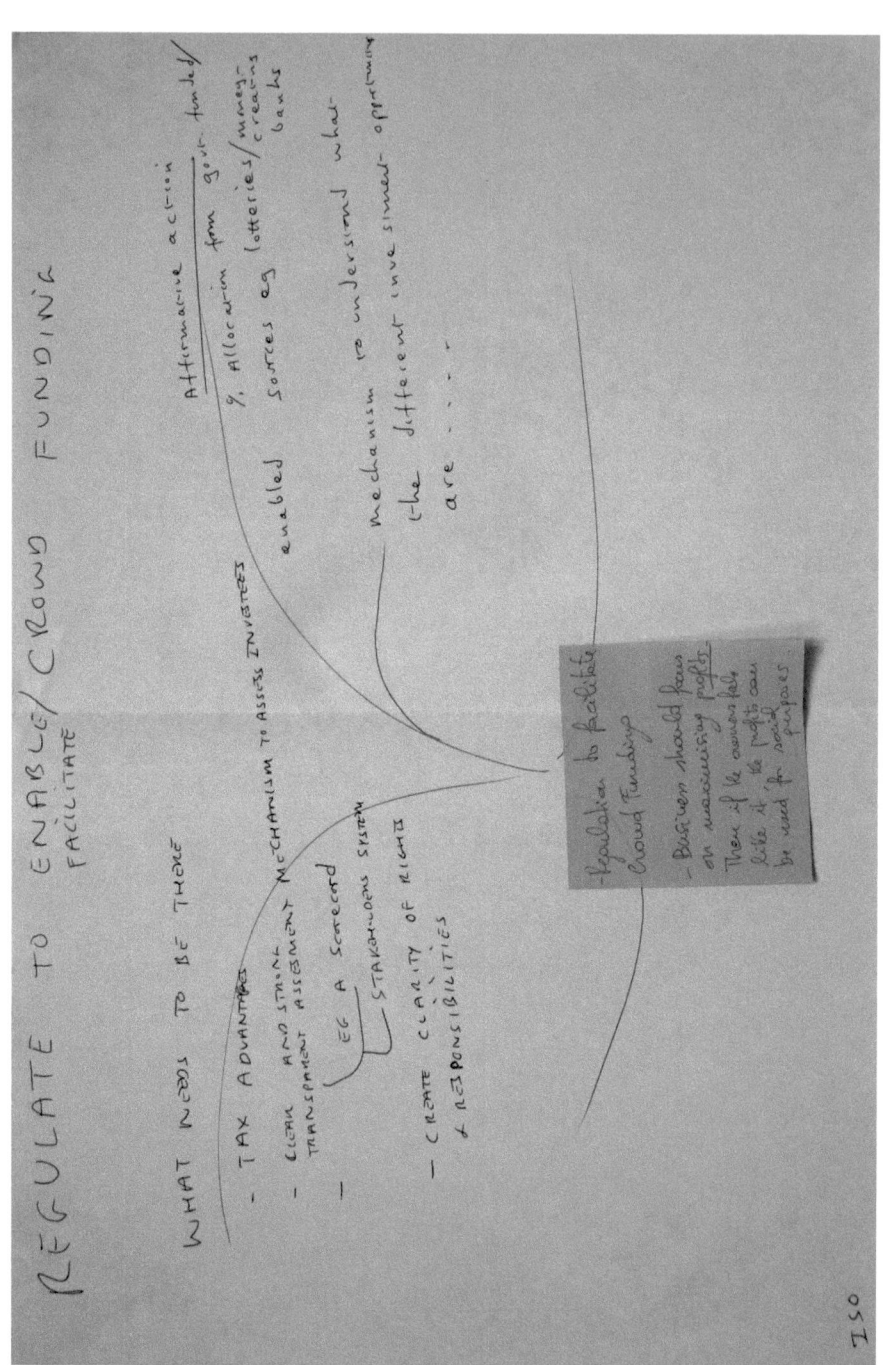

Group 3: Crowdfunding

III: Berlin Focus Group Results

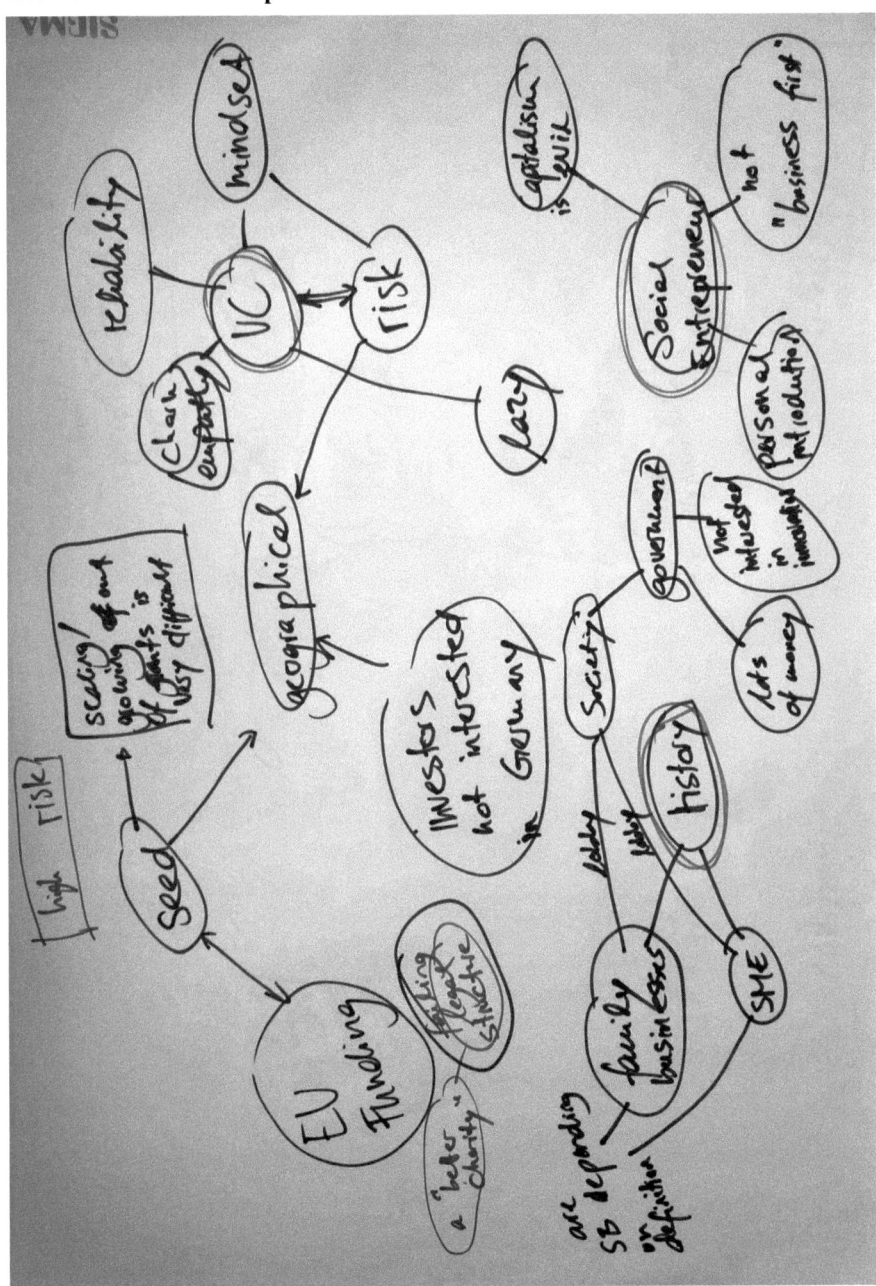

First Mindmap: Problem Areas

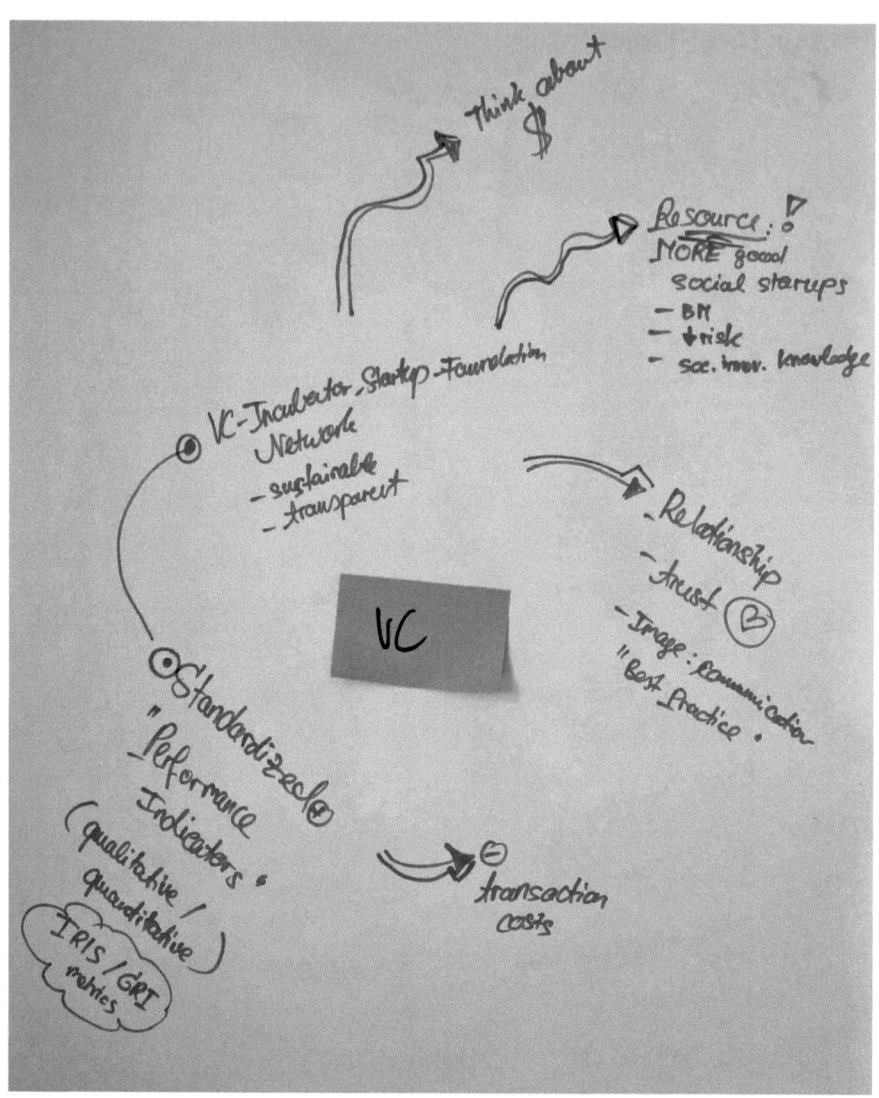

Group 1: Venture Capitalists

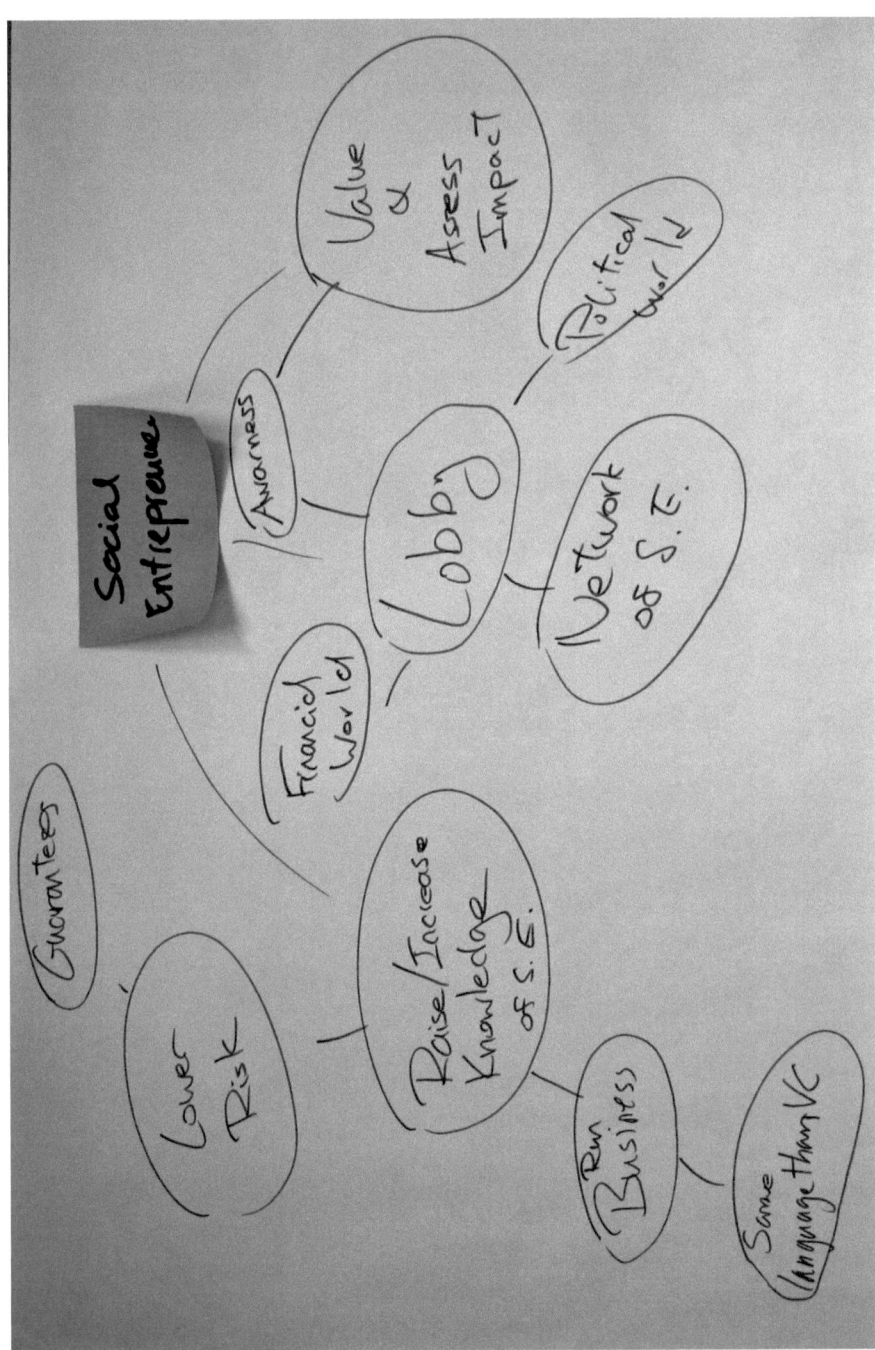

Group 2: Social Entrepreneurs

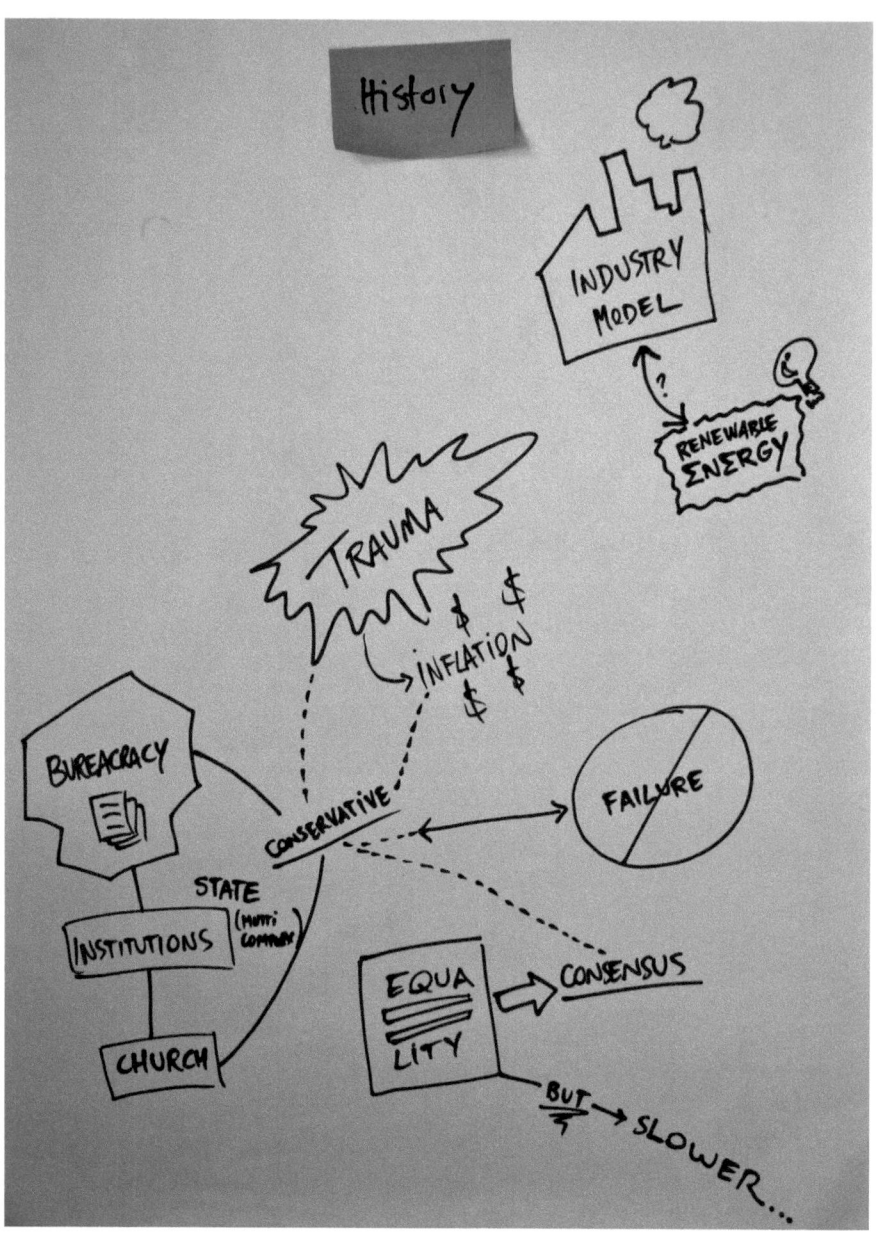

Group 3: History

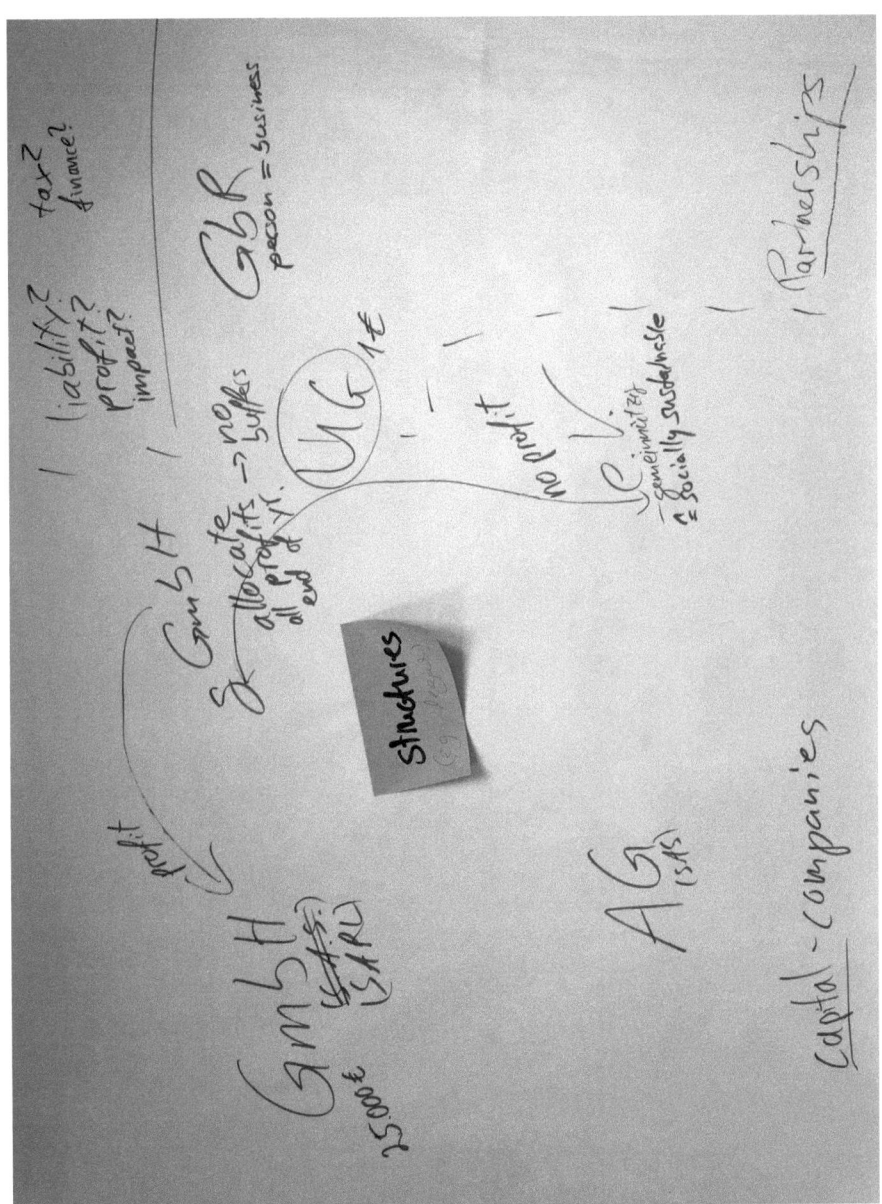

Group 4: Structures (e.g. legal)

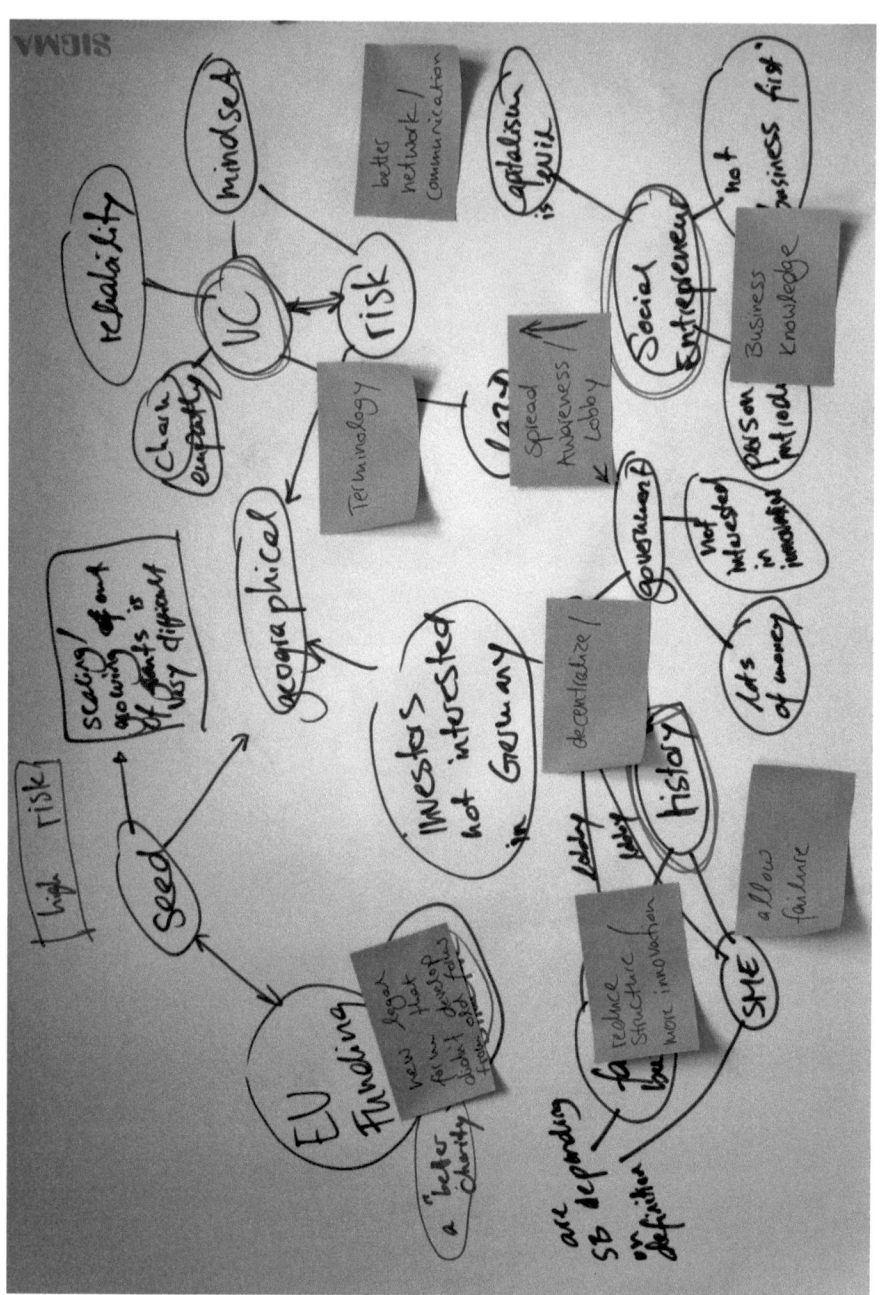

Solution ideas added to first mind-map

About the author

Laura Kromminga was born in 1989 in Berlin. She dedicated both her bachelor and master thesis to the topic of social entrepreneurship and impact investment. Previously working for the donation platform betterplace.org, the author witnessed the struggle of social organisations to raise adequate finance. Currently, she is working for the Hybrid Finance Initiative at Ashoka Europe, writing case studies and articles about Social Finance.